Leadership Connectors: Six Keys to Developing Relationships in Schools

Phyllis Ann Hensley
LaVern Burmeister

Routledge
Taylor & Francis Group
NEW YORK AND LONDON

First Published 2008 by Eye On Education

Published 2013 by Routledge
2 Park Square, Milton Park, Abingdon, Oxon OX14 4RN
711 Third Avenue, New York, NY, 10017, USA

Routledge is an imprint of the Taylor & Francis Group, an informa business

Library of Congress Cataloging-in-Publication Data

Hensley, Phyllis Ann.
Leadership connectors : developing relationships that work in schools / by Phyllis Ann Hensley and LaVern Burmeister.
p. cm.
Includes bibliographical references and index.
ISBN 978-1-59667-106-5 (alk. paper)
1. School principals—Professional relationships. 2. School personnel management. 3. Educational leadership. I. Burmeister, LaVern. II. Title.
LB2831.9.H46 2008
371.2'012—dc22
2008046894

ISBN: 978-1-59667-106-5 (pbk)

Also Available from Eye On Education

Motivating and Inspiring Teachers:
The Educational Leader's Guide for Building Staff Morale, 2nd Ed.
Todd Whitaker, Beth Whitaker, and Dale Lumpa

The High-Trust Classroom:
Raising Achievement from the Inside Out
Lonnie Moore

Creating School Cultures That Embrace Learning:
What Successful Leaders Do
Tony Thacker, John S. Bell, and Franklin P. Schargel

Applying Servant Leadership in Today's Schools
Mary K. Culver

People First!
The School Leaders' Guide to Building and Cultivating Relationships with Teachers
Jennifer Hindman, Angela Seiders, and Leslie Grant

Managing Conflict:
50 Strategies for School Leaders
Stacey Edmonson, Julie Combs, and Sandra Harris

Lead Me—I Dare You!
Managing Resistance to School Change
Sherrel Bergmann and Judith Brough

Dealing with Difficult Teachers, 2nd Ed.
Todd Whitaker

What Great Principals Do Differently:
15 Things That Matter Most
Todd Whitaker

Get Organized! Time Management for School Leaders
Frank Buck

Lead With Me: A Principal's Guide to Teacher Leadership
Gayle Moller and Anita Pankake

Professional Development: What Works
Sally J. Zepeda

Talk It Out!
The Educator's Guide to Successful Difficult Conversations
Barbara E. Sanderson

The Instructional Leader's Guide to Informal Classroom Observations, 2nd Ed.
Sally J. Zepeda

Dedication

To our husbands, Gordon Hensley and Ewald Burmeister.
You have reached the very core of our hearts and souls.
Our relationships with you make us who we are.
We are one in spirit.

Table of Contents

Preface

> Focus on the journey, not the destination. Joy is found not in finishing an activity but in doing it.
> *Greg Anderson*

Our Journey

It is interesting how and when people come together. We came together eight years ago, each having spent about 37 years in K–12 and higher education. We worked as teachers, assistant principals, principals, assistant superintendents, and superintendents. When we met, we were professors of educational leadership.

They say opposites attract; that may be why we are still good friends and continue to write and publish together. We don't look alike, dress alike, or act alike; however, we agree on certain foundational values and have developed a meaningful, purposeful, and long-lasting relationship—a friendship—with each other. We communicate well with one another, we support and care for one another through celebrations and hardships, we foster physical and emotional safety in each other, we champion each other's competence, we continue to engage in continuous personal renewal, and, most significantly, we trust each other. We have learned to grow together professionally and also in our own separate worlds.

One of us grew up in a small town in the mountains of California. This "West Coast Girl" is quiet, relaxed, pensive, calm, and reflective, yet decisive. She is gentle, respectful, and respected. She thoroughly enjoyed helping and teaching others in her administrative roles, especially in her roles as principal and then superintendent. The other author is from the East Coast. She is from Pennsylvania, and her last two positions as superintendent of schools were in New York. This "East Coast Girl" is also decisive, reflective, pensive, and calm, but she doesn't hesitate to say what she is thinking. When she went to California she was a New Yorker, running full speed ahead. She is sincere and is admired for her ability to network with a variety of people. "East" meeting "West" has worked with synchronicity. Our yin and yang have brought balance to our relationship.

Why We Wrote This Book

At this writing, we have approximately 74 years collectively in education. Although there have been some bumps in the road, we have learned a lot. We are proud of our accomplishments as we reflect on all that we did and all things wonderful that seemed to just happen to us. We have worked hard at developing relationships with teachers, colleagues, supervisors, board members, parents, community, and former students. These relationships are part of our lives and part of who we are; they help to define us.

As we wrote this book, we also thought about all the mistakes we have made and how we floundered, not knowing what to do at times. We thought about relationships that could not be rescued because we, as leaders, did not communicate with, support, protect, or trust some individuals. We did not understand at the time how important it was to nurture relationships, and we certainly did not know that we lacked the knowledge, skills, and dispositions to develop those relationships.

At times during the writing of this book, we experienced opposing emotions of joy and sadness; these emotions were somewhat of a surprise to us. We saw individual faces and experienced intense joy as we relived those times when we had a positive impact on others as a result of the relationships we built. We relived the celebration of others' accomplishments as well as our own. At the same time we experienced intense sadness, reliving sleepless nights, and were amazed that wounds were once again opened, wounds we caused to others and wounds others caused to us. We cannot travel back in time and relive all those wonderful times or change all those not so wonderful times. However, we know now that when we were truly effective in our leadership roles, it was because we worked hard at developing relationships with everyone with whom we worked. We now know that leadership is all about relationships that are meaningful, purposeful, and long-lasting.

We have loved our journey as administrators and teachers. In retrospect we wish that somewhere along the road, when we were graduate students or young administrative fledglings, someone had written a book like this that focused on relationship building. We invite you to take what you know and what you are experiencing and compare your insights with what we have experienced and come to know. Together, let's think about how relationships are developed.

Introduction

It was the Monday morning following Barker High's graduation ceremony, and Jeff, Barker's principal, was happy. He felt great about having finished his first year as principal of one of the largest high schools in the city. He was also pleased that Saturday's graduation had gone so smoothly. The parents and students were ecstatic as were the teachers who attended the ceremony. Jeff felt fulfilled as a leader and looked forward to planning for the upcoming year. At 9:30 on that Monday morning the superintendent's office called and told Jeff that the superintendent wanted to see him at 10:30. At first Jeff was alarmed; had he done something wrong? Did a strong voice in the community file a complaint? Was a board member unhappy with his performance? Jeff got hold of his emotions and then smiled to himself. The superintendent was at graduation and witnessed firsthand his leadership. Jeff got in his car, turned up the radio, started to sing, and off he went to see Dr. Dillard.

When he walked into the superintendent's office, he was elated that Dr. Dillard was smiling. Dr. Dillard said, "Jeff, you have done an outstanding job as a first year principal. Please have a seat." Jeff was overwhelmed. He thought he was there to receive accolades about graduation; however, as it turned out he was there to receive accolades about the excellent job of being a first year principal at one of the toughest high schools in the city. Dr. Dillard proceeded to congratulate Jeff on all that he had done during his first year. Everything that Dr. Dillard said related to Jeff's ability to develop relationships with everyone at the school and everyone in the community. Dr. Dillard complimented Jeff on his ability to provide support to the teachers, staff, students, and parents. He told Jeff that the president of the teachers' union had indicated that Jeff was one of the few principals who made sure that teachers had the supplies and materials needed to teach effectively. According to the union president, Jeff was also able to provide the emotional support that people needed. In addition, parents had commented time and again that Jeff was willing to listen to them. They reported that their children felt safe for the first time in the high school. Teachers were aware of what was happening in the school because of Jeff's unique ability to communicate with them. His expertise and knowledge of how to turn around the high school and improve student achievement were phenomenal. Dr. Dillard was amazed that Jeff was able to do all of this and balance his personal life as well.

The initial purpose of this meeting with Jeff was to inform him that the leadership team at the school wanted to nominate him for the upcoming principal of the year award. Since that award was months away, the teachers and parents decided that they would present Jeff with a plaque at the next board meeting. Dr. Dillard asked Jeff if he would be able to attend that meeting in July. Jeff responded with a resounding, "Yes!"

Jeff was stunned. A million things ran through his mind. It had been a great year, but he didn't realize that he had done everything the superintendent had discussed. What a rewarding and remarkable compliment!

This success story is one that we hope you will experience. Jeff realized early on how important it was to his career to develop meaningful, purposeful, and long-lasting relationships with everyone in the school.

This book has been written to help you connect with people and to develop those relationships that will help you to thrive as an effective school leader who, in concert with faculty and staff, can raise student achievement. If you want to be a better communicator who brings out the best in people, if you believe people are your most important asset, and if you believe that trying to do the job alone is impossible, then this book is for you! In this book we identify **Leadership Connectors** that will enable you to achieve your goal of building strong relationships in your school. Strong relationships can lead to skyrocketing student achievement and test scores that go through the ceiling.

Readers who have a background and interest in school leadership are most likely to relate to the experiences and examples used throughout this book. These experiences are directly related to the school context and intended to support the work of school leadership; however, they apply in a broad context to all leaders. Scenarios and discussions, while focused on the school setting, can easily be applied to other work environments. To demonstrate the universality of relationship building, occasionally we include scenarios from other work settings.

This book will be of particular interest to you if you:

1. Are a leader or want to be a leader.
2. Have developed a knowledge base regarding the importance of relationship building in achieving school success, but are having difficulty putting the skills into practice.

3. Seek practical, quickly accessible information on issues related to relationship building.
4. Are new to the field of leadership and need continuing support to hone relationship building skills.
5. Are an experienced administrator moving to a new building or assignment.
6. Have difficulty changing ineffective practices in your school or organization.
7. Have identified negative/toxic cultures and negative individual relationships in your school or organization.

This book provides a model for developing and sustaining relationships that can lead to ongoing school academic success. Through stories, practical examples, and experiences taken from actual school contexts and opportunities to reflect upon your own school situation, you can personalize and operationalize the principles included in the discussion. We present specific strategies and techniques to build and nurture relationships and to solve problems that arise in everyday situations.

Organization of the Book

The work of a school leader is time consuming, challenging, and sometimes frenetic. At times this work threatens to take over one's life. This new millennium has brought new challenges for school leaders across our nation. Now, more than ever, it is imperative that leaders initiate and cultivate communication, support, trust, a safe environment, and competence within their school cultures. Because of the demands placed on school leaders today, continuous renewal becomes even more important than it has been in the past.

In this book we introduce you to what we call **Leadership Connectors**. There are six **Leadership Connectors**, which are: **Communication, Support, Safety, Competence, Continuous Renewal,** and **Trust**. All of these Leadership Connectors must function together to develop meaningful, purposeful, and long-lasting relationships. If one of these Leadership Connectors is neglected, damaged, or missing, there is a disconnect and relationships will falter. Each Leadership Connector is as important as another; they are all interrelated and interdependent.

Each chapter in this book focuses on relationships from the standpoint of one of these six Leadership Connectors. The interplay among the six is constantly reinforced. In each chapter we introduce one of the Leadership Connectors, and then we proceed to discuss each in detail. We set the stage with this discussion so that you, the reader, have a clear understanding of each Leadership Connector.

In Chapter 1, we introduce you to **Leadership Connector, Communication** and discuss its importance in developing relationships. Often administrators will say, "They just don't get it," when referring to faculty and staff. What administrators need to understand is that their words, actions, body language, response practices, listening skills, conflict management skills, and consensus building skills all impact the quality of their relationships. We ask you to question yourself as to why they don't get it. We invite you to think about the power of your words and actions, realizing that words can inspire or destroy. We examine the critical need for you to listen and think before speaking, thus enabling you to be proactive instead of reactive. We talk about why teachers meet in the parking lot to discuss what's going on in the school instead of discussing their concerns with the leader. We address the need for you to master the skills of writing, speaking, and consensus building. Your life as a leader is so much easier when you can clearly express yourself and when you include others in making important decisions.

In Chapter 2, we introduce you to **Leadership Connector, Support**. We present and invite you to think about what support is, the importance of support, locating and using resources, and school budgets. We emphasize the need to make resources available at the beginning of the year, the importance of constant communication to determine needed resources, and the critical importance of sharing budget information. We talk about the need for faculty and staff to know that they are the most important assets in the organization, and as such, they must be recognized, celebrated, and valued. We discuss the important keys of visibility, induction, isolation, and helping and welcoming new teachers. Finally, this chapter discusses ways in which the leader can support teachers in uncomfortable situations with parents and community members.

In Chapter 3, we introduce you to **Leadership Connector, Safety** and the importance of physical, emotional, and psychological safety in developing relationships. It is impossible to effectively run a school when people do not feel safe. Self-efficacy and student achievement flourish in a safe environment. In this chapter, we invite you to think about the topics of healthy social relationships, bullying, unwelcomed surprises, orderliness, routines and procedures, predictability, innovation and autonomy, and inclusiveness. We discuss the reasons why faculty and staff need to know that the leader values their safety, that the leader will let them know what they can expect of him, and conversely, will let them know what the leader expects of them. The importance of prioritizing, of compartmentalizing, and of keeping emotions in check are discussed along with understanding the roots of emotion and how to deal with them.

In Chapter 4, we introduce you to **Leadership Connector, Competence** and its importance in developing relationships. Knowing yourself, knowing how you react to things, knowing what you know and what you don't know are all critical in developing relationships. We invite you to think about topics such as keeping current, achieving personal mastery, making decisions, solving problems, understanding how to impact school culture, building self-efficacy, and practicing ethical behavior. In this chapter, we identify key skills a leader must develop in order to be competent.

In Chapter 5, we introduce you to **Leadership Connector, Continuous Renewal**. Building relationships with one's mind, body, and soul and choosing battles are critical to administrative success. We invite you to think about such topics as emotions, finding balance, family and friends, mobility, and the value of health. Knowing which battles to fight and when to retreat are stressed in this chapter, and you are encouraged to think about what reflection really means and why it is so important in your career.

In Chapter 6, we introduce you to **Leadership Connector, Trust**. Administrators often say, "You have my word," or, "You can trust me"; however, often their actions indicate the contrary. We invite you to think about topics such as respecting versus liking, honesty, caring, valuing strengths, betrayal, perceived betrayal, and respecting privacy. We examine the feelings of pain that people experience when they have been betrayed or perceive they have been betrayed.

In Chapter 7, we pull together all six **Leadership Connectors, Communication, Support, Safety, Competence, Continuous Renewal,** and **Trust**. We reflect on a leader's career in which these connectors are embedded and highlighted.

Applying the Connectors Through Conversations with the Reader

Throughout the chapters we present mini reflective scenarios that emphasize and highlight the particular Leadership Connector we are discussing. These scenarios provide opportunities for the reader to engage in reflective thought about what the leader did that resulted in positive outcomes or what the leader could have done to prevent negative outcomes. We invite you to apply what you know to these mini scenarios and simultaneously increase your knowledge and experiential bases.

In addition to the reflective scenarios interspersed within each chapter, we end each chapter with what we call "Conversations with the Reader." We begin the conversation with a positive story, "A Walk on the Bright Side," followed by reflective questions to identify what went well and how relationships were built and reinforced.

Next we take you on "A Walk on the Dark Side" and present a story in which a Leadership Connector or a number of Connectors have not been used effectively. Some of these scenarios may seem a bit extreme; nevertheless, there are lessons one can learn by reflecting on what could have been done differently. Once again we encourage you to reflect on the story and identify what went awry. Were relationships damaged and possibly destroyed? Again we pose a number of questions to guide you.

After each story we provide our analysis and identify what might have been factors in the leaders' success or failure. We then invite you to identify a similar situation in your experience and perform a similar analysis on that personal experience. This exercise encourages you to hone your personal skills of reflection and relationship building. We close each chapter with Critical Points to Remember and suggest that these become part of your daily reading to keep you on track. We invite you to come along with us, connect with us, and develop a relationship with us as you read this book.

Chapter 1

Leadership Connector, Communication

> The most important thing in communication is hearing what isn't said.
> *Marilyn Drucker*

This Is What I Really Mean

Do these comments sound familiar?

- We need better communication around here! My principal never tells us anything.
- I didn't know we were getting new textbooks. How did Ruth, next door, know?
- I don't think my principal likes me. He never talks with me the way he talks with Bill.

Might your staff make similar statements about you as a communicator? Or might they say:

- My principal is a great communicator! I'm almost never caught off guard.
- We all seem to get important information at the same time. No one is left hanging.
- It's nice to feel part of a respected and well-informed team. I know my principal cares about me and my success.

Good **Communication** is a key **Leadership Connector**. When it exists, all other Connectors have a chance to flourish; when it does not, other Connectors have little chance of success. Attention to clear communication across the school culture is a critical element of successful school leadership.

Although you may not be aware of your influence, *everything* you say and do shapes people's opinions and feelings about you and helps them to decide whether or not to work with you or to oppose you. What you wear, how you style your hair, the kind of car you drive, the orderliness of your office, your body language, your presence or absence, and even your silence communicate something about who you are and what you represent. Understanding this can inspire you to craft words and actions that send clear messages and help others to trust your leadership skills.

Communication is one of those issues everyone talks about but few examine critically. Good communication may be praised openly or it may subtly underlie the smooth workings of the school. However it manifests itself, good communication is consistently recognized in schools as a key success factor. Conversely, "poor communication" is the nebulous scapegoat people name when things don't go well. It is the catchall excuse for everything from missed appointments to broken trust. One of the most common concerns teachers express regarding their principals is "lack of communication." Clearly, sharing information well is a high priority in school culture. This is the essence of communication. Let's look in more detail at the power of good communication in developing meaningful, purposeful, and long-lasting relationships.

Language Can Inspire

Faculty and staff are always trying to "read" their leaders. Your positional power as principal motivates them to understand who you are and what you believe. After all, the principal holds the keys to their success or failure in the workplace. You assign them; you evaluate them; and you provide them with support or withhold it from them. You are the "keeper of the vision." If they understand your expectations for them, believe that the expectations are ethical, and trust that they can meet those expectations, they are more likely to support you as their leader. Your specific comments and actions can assure your colleagues that you are trustworthy and competent.

Bruce, a new principal, found this out early in his first assignment. He met with his teachers in his first faculty meeting, and Carol, the vice president of the union, asked a predictable question—"What do you expect from the teachers in this school?" Thinking about the full meeting agenda and desiring to honor his faculty's time, Bruce provided a brief comment—"I expect you to do your best as teachers"—and moved to the next item. Carol was not satisfied and pursued the issue further—"What do you mean by our 'best'? What does it look like?"

Carol's probing for concrete answers prompted Bruce to recognize that she had given him an opportunity to express his values, beliefs, and personal vision. He said, "I expect all of us to respect each other and the students as we work toward a common vision, to act with integrity, to commit to improving our work with students, and to build a sense of community. We will work together as a team to decide how to accomplish our goals." This short statement let everyone know that Bruce (a) believes in developing a common vision, (b) values respect and integrity, (c) cares about individuals and might even challenge those who don't show respect and integrity, and (d) may give everyone help with their frustrations and support for their unique ideas to help students. This principal appears to value everyone and to favor everyone working together! His future actions will confirm or deny these tentative assumptions, but it's a great beginning.

This notion that even a first time principal is the "keeper of the vision" is often difficult for a new leader to comprehend, particularly if she moves from teaching to administration in the same school. "Oh," says the principal who just yesterday was a teacher herself, "These are my good friends. We know what we represent. We'll just keep doing what we've always done together." Such an assumption may be problematic for her. Her old friends may still be cordial, but now they may begin to edit what they say and do around her. They're not sure she is the same person; after all she's switched from casual attire to suits already.

And then comes a day when she cannot share information that the old friends want. Perhaps a colleague leaves abruptly in the middle of a school year, and her friends ask why. The give and take of their old friendship always included sharing private information. However, the new administrator is now bound by confidentiality constraints to say nothing. She is an agent for the district administration and the school board. Her friends don't understand; they feel snubbed. They let her know that their relationship has changed. They think her reluctance to share information is proof that she no longer values their friendship as she once did. After all, they would have shared the information if they were in her position.

This is a predictable and potentially painful dilemma that a new leader can avoid by choosing to make her expectations clear and expressing her vision for what the school can accomplish. If she is attuned to the anxiety in the messages her colleagues are sending her way, she can begin to reassure them that although her role has changed, she still values them and will continue to support their expertise and friendship, even if she is bound to keep some information confidential. In the long run her colleagues are likely to view her integrity toward others as reassurance that it extends to them as well.

If the principal begins his career in a school that is new to him or transfers to a school with which he has no personal history, he will need to take his time listening, observing, clarifying, and learning the culture of the school, i.e., "the way we do things around here." Did they like their former principal? Did she meet their needs? If so, he may decide to continue practices that are already in place, to build on the existing vision and to make changes in consultation with his faculty and staff to honor the work they have been doing.

Did they dislike their former principal? If so, he will need a different tactic. He will need to let them know immediately that they will be safe with him, he will listen to their concerns, he will respect their problem-solving skills, and he will seek solutions with them. To confirm his humanity for them, he might take on a high visibility concern that he knows he can remedy quickly and easily, such as ensuring that adequate supplies are always available for everyone, not just a favored few, or holding efficient staff meetings that stick to an agenda. Tackling such high profile issues can reassure his new staff right away that he is a worthy supervisor who acts on his words. With such simple actions he can set the tone for later more complex issues.

A caution here: What a leader accomplished at her last school may have been incredible and may even be the reason she was hired in the new school. She will naturally compare her experiences at the new school with her experiences at the last school—that's how we learn—but this is the new school. Telling the new faculty and staff that the previous faculty and staff did something another way may be heard as, "They did it *better* than you do." To avoid these negative interpretations, the leader can focus on issues prompted by a need the current faculty and staff demonstrate and introduce previously successful ideas without references to the last school. This allows the leader to work with current colleagues to develop a solution unique to the school. The reasoning here is akin to comparing your serious oldest child with your comedic younger child—they may both find great success in life, but the paths they follow to achieve it will be different.

Good Communication Is What?

Good communication is a complex, idiosyncratic, and sometimes subtle human process. It depends on synchronizing three channels of communication: oral, written, and nonverbal. When you are in a position of power, people pay close attention to what you say, what you write, and how you look and gesture. These are the channels you use knowingly or unknowingly to show people what you think and what you believe. *Good* communication is most likely to result when you take care to develop clear, consistent connections among (a) the information you want to communicate, (b) the language you use to communicate your message, (c) the channels you select for transmitting the message, and (d) what the receiver perceives the message to mean. For example, if a leader believes teachers can improve student achievement, he must speak it and write it using words that others will find credible and specific, and he must affirm that the information is true through his nonverbal cues and behaviors. All parts of the messaging process must be in sync. His body language and actions must verify his spoken or written message or the receiver is likely to misunderstand, distrust, or disbelieve his message.

Let's look for a moment at the statement, "People in this school are highly capable of raising student achievement." The principal may believe this with all of her heart, but it has little chance of coming to pass if she cannot transmit this belief to teachers (a) so they believe that she believes it and (b) so they believe it about themselves.

Following is a possible scenario for how a leader might immerse everyone in the message throughout the school day, making it more likely that the receivers will hear the message as she intends:

She might begin by making the statement—"I know that people in this school are highly capable of raising student achievement"—in a faculty meeting, including some evidence of why she believes it. The evidence might include comments like:

- "I know you can do it because you have raised test scores beyond the target number each of the last three years."
- "A mother caught me in the hall last week to say how much her daughter is learning with the new fourth grade team. She comes home and teaches the whole family what she just learned in math that day!"
- "I was so excited to come to this school because I heard about the commitment of this staff, and I wanted to be a part of it. High school faculty and staffs are not famous for working together, but I heard that you have a strong team here."

She could then visit classrooms regularly, noticing the individual actions teachers take to support student achievement. A quick note left on the desk will verify what she has noticed, and a *warm, sincere* smile will provide nonverbal confirmation of her written words that might include:

- "Stephen is so engrossed in his work. What a turnaround from last year! How did you do it?"
- "I didn't want to leave before you finished the lesson. Your students were so focused on your instruction they never even noticed that I was in the room."
- "Your explanation of the writing process inspired me to think more about revising my work before I have others read it. Thanks!"

If she observes weaknesses, the leader might make note of them to address face-to-face with individual teachers at a later time. Her current goal is to foster a positive tone of respect throughout the school culture. Hence, she will avoid the human tendency to focus on the negative, to try to "fix" things.

If she thinks a teacher would feel complimented by her actions, she might run to the front of the room and interrupt class, asking, "Do you know that your teacher is the best in the world?" Of course, like the serious older child, some teachers might be paralyzed with embarrassment by this outburst, so she could whisper the same words to the quiet girl in the back row and ask her to pass it on. When the principal leaves a similar message for every teacher in a personal way, it confirms that she believes in everyone so strongly that she is willing to tell another person about the teacher's competence. She is sending the message that she is trustworthy.

A cautionary note to this scenario: Some schools have cultures that do not support pop-in visits to classrooms. For some reason—a critical observer, personal feelings of inadequacy, lack of precedent—the faculty may not yet be comfortable with the practice. If the leader is to develop a positive school culture in which people view each other as supportive colleagues, then it is wise to gradually build trust in the process of popping in and noticing good teaching practices. A good starting place is to begin with the most competent and confident teachers and to extend the opportunity to others as positive word spreads. The leader may need to prep people in the beginning and make visits short until the teacher reaches a high enough comfort level. If care is taken, even the most intense high school teacher will cherish his stash of positive notes from the principal!

The principal might transmit the same message to her administrative assistant, saying:

- "The time you spent with Johnny, helping him to sit quietly in the office waiting for his mother makes him feel that we all care about him. Thank you."

To the custodian:

- "Your obsession with clean bathrooms tells students that you respect them and teaches them to respect themselves and their surroundings. This respect will carry over into their learning. Thank you."

To the PTA or Booster Club president:

- "Raising money for field trips has helped our students to see their learning come alive in the real world. It makes a huge difference. Thank you."

To the cafeteria worker:

- "You work so hard to help students choose healthy food for lunch. That helps them to think better all afternoon—even during the last class of the day. Thank you."

Soon everyone will believe that this school can be improved and that the resources lie in the people who work here. Over time this positive belief will develop roots and branches. In this developing climate of trust, the faculty and staff can begin the hard work of asking themselves what is working, what they are doing well, alone and together, and what needs to be changed. They will feel ready to examine their practice in a supportive environment.

On the other hand, a leader can also sabotage success by claiming that, "People in this school are highly capable of raising student achievement" and then sending conflicting written and/or nonverbal messages. She could, for example, emulate the English teacher who cannot live without his red pen, and write short *critical* notes as she enters the classroom. Of course, in the principal's mind, she would only be helping the teacher to remedy weaknesses, but the teacher is likely to view her *helpful* comments as contradictory to her stated belief that all teachers are capable. The principal's critical written message speaks louder than her words because the teacher can read the written message over and over again. The oral praise disappears in the wind, overshadowed by the written note. Then, if the leader's body language is stiff and unsmiling, she further confirms the written message. It is human nature to cling to the negative when contradictory messages appear. "Aha," listeners say, "We knew it was too good to be true—you say you believe in us, but you can't wait to criticize us." Effective communication is sincere. This sincerity leads to consistency across all channels of communication—spoken words, written words, and actions.

Administrators Say the Craziest Things

One day Carl, a middle school principal, complained to his spouse that he had said the dumbest thing to someone at lunch and created a huge problem. "Why didn't I think before I spoke?" he asked. "Why didn't I listen more carefully?" he lamented. "The mess could have been cleaned up so quickly if only I . . ., What was I thinking? I guess I wasn't thinking." On and on went the self-pummeling!

School administration is a busy, often hectic, career. It provides fertile ground for gaffs, goofs, and self-criticism. A sense of humor can often disarm an awkward or tense situation and the resulting personal angst. A quick quip or a hearty laugh is well worth cultivating to ease tensions and allow frustrations to fade away. For a sense of personal balance and for the same gift to others, use your sense of humor. Laughing at your own mistakes reassures others that they will be forgiven for their slips as well.

However, sometimes a sense of humor is not the tool to use. It cannot carry a leader through every situation in which he or she should have listened and taken time to think. Taking time and using the tools necessary to *receive* messages is as important as *sending* clear messages. When we send a message, we must choose our words with honesty and sincerity so that our gestures can naturally add to the clarity of the message and affirm our comments. Our gestures betray us if we don't believe the message we are sending.

When we receive a message, we must listen to be sure that we understand the sender's intention. Then we must ask questions to clarify any confusion *before* we respond with words or actions. If our minds are already made up about the actions we will take, others will sense an inconsistency between our words and our body language. Above all, when the communication system breaks down, we must apologize for our mistakes and accept apologies from others when they offer them.

Here is an example of how easily a leader's words can be misinterpreted if his body language sends a conflicting message. When Hugo, a high school principal, complained that he had two teachers who never seemed to understand and follow his directions, a colleague told him that she makes a point of saying, "Help me understand . . .," to get clarification in a confusing situation. She sincerely wants to understand and believes that the teacher can help her to do so. Hugo just laughed at her saying, "*You* can say that, and it works for you. I could never say that. Teachers would take one look at my body language and hear my words as sarcasm." Hugo understood that body language would surely betray him if he did not speak with sincerity, and the truth was he really didn't want to understand; he just wanted the behavior to stop. What a simple confirmation that a technique that works for one leader may flop for another. A leader needs to think about what he or she really wants to accomplish and then choose the language to convey the message clearly.

Frame It!

Choosing language allows a leader to "frame" or adjust the spin on a situation. Every situation is "framed" in some manner. That is, it is described using specific words and actions that provide a lens through which people can process the message. The media are often accused of using framing or spinning in a negative way to persuade people that a news event or political belief is right or wrong. Framing is a powerful tool to achieve a vision and must be used with integrity. A leader can frame a situation as a catastrophe or as a noble challenge, as a problem or as an opportunity. Framing the situation as an opportunity automatically moves it out of the shadows and into a positive light. It evokes the human desire to believe that this is an achievable challenge rather than a hopeless quagmire.

A story is told in various versions about a little girl frantically shoveling piles of manure out of an incredibly soiled barn. When asked what she is doing, she replies, "I'm sure there is a pony in here somewhere. I just need to keep digging until I find it." This child is a masterful framer of information. To her the manure indicates that a wonderful possibility lies in front of her. A more cynical framer would complain that the manure is nothing more than a smelly heap that requires extensive physical labor to remove. The situation is the same, but the interpretations of what is and what could be are vastly different between the two frames.

Like the little girl, some administrators seem to transmit hope even in bleak situations. Ella is one of those people. Ella was a 4th year middle school principal with a teacher on her faculty who struggled daily to manage his beginning Spanish class. She knew there was a strong possibility that she would recommend the teacher not be rehired for the next year. Her state only required notification to a probationary teacher by March of the year of nonreelection with no further explanation, but Ella was not comfortable with this process. She began to meet with the teacher, observing his strengths and providing guidance to strengthen his weaknesses. She visited his classroom regularly and then met with him to solicit his concerns and offer appropriate assistance. As she got to know him better, she discovered that he had always wanted to be a translator for the United Nations. She encouraged him to pursue his dream as she continued to support his improvement in the classroom. By March, she was not ready to offer a contract for the next year. The teacher still struggled with his classes, but the relationship of genuine caring she had nurtured with the teacher made it easier for her to inform him. Her encouragement of the teacher's dream led him to seek UN employment. When she told him he would not be invited to return, he was able to thank her for her push to take a risk and tell her how excited he was to be starting his lifelong wish to translate for the UN that summer.

This scenario may not be typical, and it is time consuming. Ella would have been justified in turning the situation over to a department chair or mentor teacher and stepping away except for the final decision. A leader cannot do everything, nor should she, but for Ella this was a priority. She knew that word of her sincere kindness to a struggling teacher would spread across the school culture and make trusting, purposeful relationships possible with everyone. She was able to frame even a dismissal situation as an opportunity!

Other administrators may be more cynical and even accusatory, leaving the dismissed teacher in emotional shambles. A hopeful administrator is likely to frame the situation as an opportunity, a challenge to be pursued; a cynical administrator may frame the situation as a disaster that only dismissal can solve. Let's try a few examples in which you imagine yourself as the administrator in the situation.

You have just discovered that your test scores are the lowest in the district. After your initial reactions of embarrassment, finding someone to blame, screaming unfairly at your spouse, and deciding that you are not cut out to be an administrator after all, try reframing the situation. Begin the clarification process, the inquiry, the quest. If nothing else, a quest can pique your interest without assigning blame. You are simply gathering data and then beginning to process it like an experienced investigator. It quiets your initial angry, embarrassed responses and sets you on the path toward reframing. Hope builds. Now you are eager to sleuth out anything that will enlighten the situation. You can then formulate some questions like the following and invite others, perhaps a leadership team, to join you in the investigation:

- What do you know about what has worked?
- Is there a group of students who did exceptionally well?
- Who are they, and what do they have in common?

- Can you find ways to do more of what worked with these students?
- What little success stories lurk inside individual teachers' and students' experiences with the test?

If you discover something along the way that is slightly or even terribly in need of revision or elimination, decide with those who will be affected by it how to make necessary changes.

When you use this positive approach, even the most ingrained practices can be eliminated if they prove to be ineffective. You are creating a school focused on illumination, not on missteps in the darkness, a school that names its strengths and tackles its weaknesses without excuses, setting a path to overcome them.

Or suppose your leadership team chair, the teacher who models positive actions for the rest of the staff, is moving to another district. You are sure that this will totally disrupt all of the fledgling plans you are laying with your leadership team to build a positive school culture, a learning community. She is the heart and the inspiration for the project. Pause for a moment to listen to sad music, cry a little, or run 20 miles if you must; then get on with the reframing. Ask yourself:

- What is the legacy she is leaving?
- What work is already in place?
- What can be built upon?
- Who can be tapped to fill the void?
- Who will now have the opportunity to shine?
- Is it one person or perhaps several people who would not have been noticed if the shining star had stayed?

Reframing offers the opportunity to build on what works, not to lament what you cannot control. It offers the opportunity to be proactive rather than reactive. It changes hopelessness into hopefulness. Communicating your hopeful view of the situation with others will help them to find hope as well.

A word of caution about all this hope is that a large gap between your hopefulness and others' despair can be difficult to cross if the distance is too great. Building bridges of reassurance and support can help you to avoid appearing naïve and "Pollyannaish."

One day Carlos asked Janene, his principal, to stop giving him "opportunities." Janene had consistently framed what he called problems as opportunities. Carlos said he was tired of all these new opportunities. But Janene noticed that he expressed his weariness with a smile. This was a new persona for this neurotic professional who lived in constant fear that his performance was never good enough. Since the introduction of "opportunities," he had taken on many challenges that he would never have attempted in the past. In reframing, Janene never minimized Carlos's real concerns or ignored his real needs. On the contrary, the reframing allowed him to do the hard work of identifying challenges and developing ways to meet them without the excessive anxiety that would have posed a barrier.

Of course, this is the real world, and sometimes your best efforts won't "fix" an inadequate, negligent, or incompetent teacher. Be prepared to hold tightly to your vision in this situation and consider that you may need to work through documentation, assistance plans, mentoring, etc., to remove those who sabotage the shared vision of providing the best education for every student in your school. In his groundbreaking work, *Good to Great* (2001), Jim Collins reminded us that it is critical to have the right people on the bus, and then to let them do their jobs. Hiring the right people in the first place is the best answer, but replacing those who seriously hinder the vision is just as critical.

Why Are They Meeting In The Parking Lot?

Every administrator has surely experienced closing a staff meeting and then noticing small groups gathering—often in the parking lot. What are they talking about? In some cases it is innocent talk of the moment: They haven't seen each other for awhile, and they are catching up; they have had something on their minds that they haven't had the time to discuss with friends; they saw the greatest movie; someone is newly pregnant, etc. But questions are always worth asking:

- Was something unresolved in your meeting that is concerning one or more teachers?
- Is there a new idea that someone was reluctant to mention during the meeting?
- Do you have a rabble-rouser in the midst?
- Does someone have a personal concern about you?
- Have you done something that offended someone?

Body language can give you some clues—open spaces in the group, smiles, and waves indicate that all is well. On the other hand, huddling together, hands cupping around words, and eyes scanning the area for eavesdroppers suggest that you should investigate a bit. Nonverbal communication can help you to understand your staff just as your nonverbal communication can help them to understand you. Learn to use it. If you have a hunch that something is amiss, you are probably right. Current research suggests that our emotional centers work much quicker than our cognitive centers. The emotional centers cue us to flee or to relax well before our rational brains kick in to analyze our feelings. Therefore, you should pay attention to your hunches and follow up on them, but don't let them lead you into a place where you act without thought.

One way to get more information before acting is to ask a trusted teacher what he has noticed. Ask him to tell you if there is a situation brewing that you should address. Then be willing to listen, think, and do something about it. People appreciate being recognized as competent and trustworthy and most will go far beyond expectations to help clarify issues and improve them. When the leader follows through with integrity, respecting those who may have concerns and the person who has helped to discover the concerns, problems become opportunities.

I Never Could Write Very Well

Thus far we have talked about (a) recognizing the importance of consistency in oral, written, and nonverbal language; (b) sending clear messages and clarifying messages sent to you; (c) understanding the power of reframing situations to instill hope rather than despair; (d) recognizing that communication requires listening and thinking; and (e) paying attention to your hunches. These guidelines affect both a leader's oral and written messages. If a leader knows that what he says, writes, and does is always under scrutiny, then he must take care to send a consistent message through all channels—including writing. It is human nature to look for slips and slides that can be criticized and used as evidence that all is not well. A very literal example of this phenomenon lies in the tendency to judge a person's competence by her grammatical usage and spelling. The leader could write an exceptionally welcoming letter to parents, but if he misspells or misuses one word, that word may obscure the meaning of the whole message for the reader whose attention is riveted on the misspelling. Perhaps nowhere other than in spelling and grammar does American culture judge its leaders so harshly. Teachers, parents, students, and the community expect perfection when it comes to written communication. It is particularly important with the chief educator in the school. A slip on his part gives staff permission to send sloppy, poorly proofed and edited letters home. Such letters damage public perception of school quality.

So what should a leader do if he tends to slip in a "*there*" where a "their" should be on occasion or "weird" often comes out as "*wierd*?" First, use the spelling and grammar check feature on the computer, and, second, enlist a proofreader for everything sent to others! The leader should read what he has written out loud to himself and/or have someone read what he has written out loud to him.

It is not necessary to write creatively, scholarly, or poetically; it *is* necessary to write competently, clearly, and coherently. If a leader's university papers came back with marks chastising his grammar, usage, spelling, consistency, coherence, clarity, etc., he might consider taking a writing class or, at the very least, having friendly eyes read what he writes before he sends it to a more general audience. Even humor doesn't work when a leader is trying to explain what others perceive as sloppy thinking, or worse, incompetence. The message itself is hard enough to transmit so others understand it as the leader intends without asking readers to leap the barrier of poor writing as well.

The Email

Let us consider two methods of communication that rely on good writing skills—email and newsletters—and offer some suggestions for getting the best value from each.

Email is free and efficient. Many schools have the capability to send a quick email to every teacher with one click, assuring that everyone gets the same message at the same time (depending of course on how often the teachers read their emails). The messages require only basic computer skills. These are wonderful advantages that make the temptation to use email irresistible; however, a leader must be careful. Following are a few guidelines to develop relationships with individual teachers and staff through email:

- Keep messages short and to the point.
- Check spelling, grammar, and punctuation. Some people are bothered by casual writing such as writing the entire email in lower case, signing names in lower case, and using "i" instead of "I."
- Use a conversational style.
- Send kudos and "atta-boys" but *not* criticisms. Develop faculty and staff expectations that an email from you will lift rather than depress their spirits. Reserve critical comments and concerns for face-to-face discussions where you can watch the body language of the listener and correct any misunderstandings as you go along.

- Consider dropping in short, kind comments that show your concern for each recipient. Such comments can allow you to build personalized relationships through email. Let your voice shine to show people that you appreciate them.
- Remember that mistakes happen in sending emails—they somehow get lost, or they go to the wrong person(s)—so do not assume that the person got the message and avoid writing anything that you wouldn't want the world to see. Once you push "send," you cannot retrieve it!
- Send important messages through multiple or more formal channels.
- Maintain two email addresses—one for personal messages and one for professional correspondence. Use work email for work-related items only.

The Newsletter

Newsletters can be more than a simple list of announcements to parents. They offer an opportunity to enlist others in a vision of success for the school. Here are some guidelines for using them to their greatest advantage:

- Keep the articles current with new information that cannot generally come from other sources.
- Know your audience and their interests, and write to draw them in.
- Edit for content, clarity, grammar, spelling, coherence, and style.
- Use a readable font and supportive graphics and pictures.
- Write as if you can hardly wait to tell the news. Let your voice shine.
- Follow up on previous issues.
- Ask yourself if everything included in the newsletter somchow supports your school vision and goals.

Technical Writing

Another type of writing that a leader needs to perfect is the technical writing required for school plans, grants, applications, etc. To succeed at writing these kinds of documents, we suggest that you:

- Read the requirements several times and address *each* one separately.
- Frame problems as opportunities or challenges you are excited to tackle wherever possible.

- Find similar documents written by others and observe the style and format.
- Use clear, positive, succinct language. Include examples when appropriate.
- Volunteer to help an accomplished writer prepare a document so you can develop your own skill.
- Ask multiple readers to comment on the written document before submission.
- Remember that evaluators of these documents are following the same guidelines you followed. They may bypass your statements on each point if you embed them in a slick narrative. Make your statements explicit.

Writing is a powerful tool to reveal the real person to other people and to foster a consistent vision of success that people can read multiple times. A leader should take writing seriously. His competence and integrity are affirmed or denied in every informal or formal piece he authors. Becoming a skillful writer is worth the effort.

Consensus Building—It Makes My Life So Much Easier

Consensus building is hard, time-intensive work. It requires everyone involved to ponder an issue from multiple perspectives. For this reason, people must know that a leader will only ask them to go through the consensus building process on significant, purposeful, ethically acceptable issues that are critical to achieving the vision of the school. In other words, an issue considered for consensus must be important to the work the leader and the team are doing as a group.

When building consensus, a group honors a diversity of beliefs and opinions on an issue, trying to find the common ground. Consensus is not the same as compromise in which the ideas of some may be diminished or sacrificed in order to achieve agreement. Consensus asks the group to consider all ideas, discussing benefits and shortcomings of each. Often the outcome of dialogue leading to consensus is a course of action that combines or synthesizes many perspectives. Such a dialogue may reveal a new way of approaching an issue that no one originally identified. It is *in*clusive, not *ex*clusive. Clear communication provides the groundwork for the process.

Consensus depends on dialogue, an open give and take of ideas in which participants attempt to broaden their understanding of an issue. This contrasts with "compromise" which may depend more on debate in which participants attempt to persuade others to accept their points of view. Consensus building engages people in thinking critically, in expressing tentative ideas or criticisms, in listening to others' ideas and blending them with their own. It can be a highly creative process, satisfying to everyone who participates. Successful consensus building requires respect and trust among participants and rises from an ethical vision they hold in common. In return the group develops deeper respect, trust, and commitment to the goal.

Consensus building is integral to relationship building, and relationship building is the key to developing and maintaining successful schools. Sometimes administrators appear to engage in consensus building and put on a good show of it, knowing they are going to do what they want to do anyway. Be aware that teachers know what leaders such as these are doing and might talk about that in the parking lot also.

Steps to Achieving Consensus

You may already know that consensus building is important but wonder how you can accomplish it. What does it take to build consensus? The response is complex, but here are ideas to consider that can get the process going.

A leader needs to recognize that every decision doesn't require a formal consensus process. In fact the faculty and staff will expect the leader to make everyday decisions on his own and protect them from issues that don't concern them directly. This is a key point. A leader may frustrate or irritate people if he tries to involve them in every decision. The consensus process should be reserved for important issues that impact the school vision because the process takes time and effort to accomplish well.

Ideally, the leader should invite people who have a personal interest and expertise in an issue to participate in a consensus building session. Others may feel confused or irritated if they are invited. For example, English teachers care very much about the textbooks they choose to teach English and have the expertise to choose just the right ones, but a math teacher would be nonplussed by an invitation to join the English teachers in selecting the English texts.

If the people involved in the process have a personal interest in an issue but lack expertise, the leader will need to find ways to provide the expertise for them. "Shared ignorance" is frustrating for people because they tend to wallow in existing conditions with no way to progress. On the other hand, a person with expertise and no personal interest in the issue may be most effective as an advisor to the process without fully participating.

Whenever possible, the leader should include only people who are committed to the vision and goals of the school and who will consider the issue under discussion critically, based on what is best for the organization. If on occasion the leader must include a hostile person, he can surround her with strong voices that can reframe her negativity while still considering her concerns. Sometimes such opposing perspectives can clarify the issue at hand and identify some previously unconsidered points. The leader will need to monitor the work of the group and remove the agitator only as a last resort.

People expect the leader to be honest about the decision-making power of the group. If the group will make the final decision based on a consensus, he should say so; if the group will be advisory only, he should let the members know when they begin their work. People get frustrated if they think the group has decision-making power, and then they discover after extensive work that their decision will be overturned by a higher authority or that the leader is going to do it his way anyway.

The leader should understand that each group is likely to go through specific stages to become a viable, working team. They will need time to (a) be polite and make small talk, much like attendees at a cocktail party, (b) define their roles within the group, (c) establish procedures and routines for the group to follow, and (d) define the task and complete the work they are expected to do.

The leader must oversee the process to assure that the group moves efficiently through each of these stages. There is potential for bogging down at any stage, and his ability to recognize that the behaviors within each stage are normal but must be moved forward will help the group members to accomplish their goals. The group will get to the task sooner and stick to it if the task is clear, achievable, and perceived to be important to the shared vision of the group.

Group Pitfalls

A leader wants the group to respect and trust one another, to seek clarification and evidence in lively dialogues, and to develop a clear yet flexible plan to address the issue(s). She must be watchful of a group that develops one or more of the following attributes or behaviors because the group may bog down and fail to accomplish its tasks. These attributes tend to lead to "groupthink," an uncritical, lazy approach to the task:

- The group members begin to stick together on everything and defend their position without justification, or they begin to build a cocoon, shutting outsiders out. They will need a leader to help them revisit their procedures and routines to assure that they critically examine the issue.
- Group members may begin to show signs of obeisance, allowing the ideas of a charismatic group member to reign unchallenged. The leader will need to help the group to revise their procedures to allow everyone to participate fully.
- A group that cannot establish effective procedures or routines may flail and flounder. The leader will need to guide the members toward establishing workable routines and procedures. Providing models may help.
- A group may be too homogeneous to generate varied ideas. Four young, married women with small children who have only taught second grade or six male physical education teachers who have coached football for ten seasons together may be too like-minded to think critically about an issue together. They may need someone with diverse ideas to challenge their unexamined beliefs. The leader may need to revise the membership of the group, or better yet, create diverse groups at the beginning. Once formed, a group tends to develop an identity and become resistant to changing members. Changing the group membership can move a group back to ground zero and necessitate moving through all the stages of group development again, but such a delay may be necessary if the group is floundering.
- A group that feels pressure from external sources may rush to complete the work and sacrifice critical analysis in the process. The pressure could come from such sources as angry parents waiting for resolution of an issue or from a school board deadline. Group members will need their leader to help calm their anxiety before they can focus on the work.
- A group that has suffered recent failure, feels confused about the task, faces an ethical dilemma, etc., may struggle with rising to the challenge. They will need clarification, reassurance that they are competent, and encouragement to focus on the task.

If a leader sees evidence of these attributes or behaviors developing in a group, he may need to step in to help with problem-solving strategies. If he misses or ignores the signs, he may see unproductive mindsets take control of the group. These mindsets sabotage the work, and the leader will need to intervene to get the group back on track.

When a leader is watchful and helps the groups slide past the obstacles, the consensus process can be a fulfilling and energizing experience. It validates human ability and creativity, allows social needs to be met, and leads to high quality outcomes. Observe the cautions and enjoy the ride.

Conversations with the Reader

A Walk on the Bright Side

Now it's your turn. Read the following story, and reflect on the ways effective **Leadership Connector, Communication** is demonstrated. See the questions at the end of this story to guide your reflection.

Martin

Martin had spent his entire 18-year teaching career in secondary classrooms—never a minute in an elementary setting. But there he was with his first assignment as a principal—at an elementary school. He knew he had no credibility with staff in this assignment, so he vowed to be the best listener and learner he could be. During the first staff meeting, he humbly told his staff about the areas in which he had expertise (curriculum planning, teaching strategies, reading instruction, special education, connections to secondary grades teaching, and building relationships with people) and the obvious areas in which he was excited to learn from them. He told them he was committed to learning everything they were willing to teach him. He wandered the classrooms, encouraging teachers to teach him all about what they taught and how they taught it. He left notes every time he went in, thanking them for what he had learned that day and appreciating the expertise he observed. He smiled often because it was a rare treat to have so many highly capable professionals as his mentors.

Occasionally, he had trouble finding the positive in a classroom, but his goal was to build rapport and trust, so he commented on bulletin boards that supported a lesson objective when there was nothing else to note.

He told a story to kindergarteners, trying to ignore the tiny hands clasped around his knees as he spoke. He laughed with the teacher when he realized that his story was too long for wiggly five-year-olds. He told a story he didn't much like to a fifth grade class and decided with the teacher's help that he would be much more effective if he came back and told a story that he really liked. The plan worked, and he rejoiced with the teacher.

He asked the special education teacher to teach him how to safely restrain a rude and combative third grade boy. She did, and then they laughed together over Martin's bruised legs. Apparently, he had not mastered the leg restraining technique. The teacher re-taught him, and Martin was successful the next time.

He empathized with an exemplary teacher's tearful complaints that her grade-level colleagues were cruel to her and critical of her effective teaching methods. He walked the playground at lunch time, learning children's names and play habits. He substituted in teachers' classrooms so they could meet with upset parents or spend time planning with colleagues. He learned about elementary school, about HIS elementary school, by watching, listening, empathizing, and appreciating.

Over time he became competent enough and trusted enough to ask some questions that started meaningful conversations:

- How do you know that Johnny is progressing at an appropriate rate?
- Who is your most able student and who is your least able?
- How did you decide who is most able and who is least able?
- How are you supporting each?
- What teaching strategies work best for your students?
- Where would you like to see more success?

The questions were designed for individual teachers and rose from the context of their own classrooms. He didn't have a set questioning routine. He was simply asking questions that arose when he was observing teachers at their craft.

Karen was a master at teaching math. Martin's questions for her were based on what she was doing to teach these kids so effectively. How did she set up her groups? What were the criteria for placing certain students together? How did she know when to move on? What did she do when a child got stuck? Her answers to his questions gave Martin responses to questions other teachers were asking. He was becoming a bee engaged in pollinating flowers. After pondering, he recommended one teacher to another as having a possible answer to a classroom quandary. He tried to include everyone as an expert in some way—some were great organizers, some were fantastic all-around teachers, some had only minimal skills, but all had something to give and share with others.

Sometimes he sensed a need to back off, not to set one teacher up as an expert, and then he would search further for those who had not been recognized as often as others. Jerry was having little success with helping his students to improve as readers, but he was fantastic with classroom management and getting a whole class of first graders to the cafeteria in a line. Martin drew on Jerry's skills, and in turn Jerry became receptive to others who were having more success with reading instruction. Within two years Jerry's student progress was right up there with other first grades.

When Martin noticed at the end of the year that writing samples for fourth grade were not as strong as those for second grade, he knew just how to proceed. Because of an open flow of communication, he had the trust and support of staff, and he knew that he could begin to focus questions on what was working in writing instruction. Then he could structure groups to ask themselves critical questions for improvement. He decided that this elementary principalship was actually a pretty good gig!

Reflective Questions

1. How would you describe Martin's approach to communicating with his new staff?
2. Do you think the communication in this story happened by accident or by design? Explain.
3. What worked? What puzzled you?
4. What did Martin do that could transfer to your situation?
5. What would you do differently from Martin? Why?
6. If you had a chance to talk to Martin, what would you say or ask?
7. Describe how relationships were built or damaged.

Our Analysis

Martin is humble, teachable, and sincere, and his words and actions verified these attributes. He framed his first assignment as a principal as an adventure he was excited to undertake rather than as a daunting duty to endure until he could apply for a secondary position. He let his certificated and classified staff know in multiple ways that he appreciated their expertise and expected to learn from them. This had the immediate effect of reducing their stress and inspiring them to concentrate on doing an even better job. Martin took risks that could have made him look incompetent, but his sense of humor and willingness to acknowledge his mistakes let others know that it was safe to make and learn from mistakes on their own journeys toward improvement.

Everything Martin did and said was consistent with what he believed. He communicated with honesty and synchrony. This allowed him to develop trust with colleagues. Martin's communication may appear to be a natural process, probably due to his personality, but we think it is a combination of personal characteristics and skills developed over time. Martin values people as individuals and respects their strengths. He makes positive comments about them both orally and in writing and transmits praise through third parties whenever possible; he communicates criticism in private and face-to-face whenever possible so he can clarify reasons and misconceptions.

Martin could have come to the school determined to show the staff that he was competent, masking his underlying sense of inadequacy with detailed plans for improvement or authoritarian pronouncements of changes he would make to the status quo. If he had done this, the staff may have noted the inconsistencies between his words and his body language. They may have become resentful or resistant, feeling devalued as professionals. Instead, he chose to listen and learn. The staff appreciated his honesty and began to trust him. He will make mistakes in the future, as we all do, but we think that his clear, honest communication skills will fill a reservoir of staff trust that he can draw upon when he needs it. He will be able to draw strength from the reservoir to develop a clear, articulated vision and a plan for continuous improvement with his teachers and staff and replenish the reservoir as the work shows success.

A Walk on the Dark Side

Now read the next story and reflect on what went awry. See the questions at the end of this story to guide your reflection.

Elizabeth

It was May and Elizabeth had just been appointed principal of Eastside High School for the upcoming year. She was thrilled with her new job, but Eastside's former principal did not officially retire until September 1 of that year. Although Elizabeth was appointed in May, she decided not to come to Eastside High or interact with the faculty during the summer. It was rumored that she didn't like Eastside's principal and wanted to wait until he retired to appear. Consequently, when September rolled around, faculty and support staff were concerned about being "leaderless." They proceeded with the opening of school as they had done in the past.

When Elizabeth finally came on board, she was surprised to find out that the faculty handbook had not been updated and duplicated for the academic year. Jane and Lou (chairs of the science and math departments) decided that they would roll up their sleeves and help Elizabeth. It was Thursday, and teachers were going to report back to work the following Wednesday. They called Elizabeth and offered their help. Elizabeth seemed pleased, so Jane and Lou worked the next day and the entire weekend updating and editing the faculty handbook.

These two teachers worked hard, happy they could help the new principal. Monday came, and Jane and Lou presented Elizabeth with the edited version of the handbook. Elizabeth smiled at the two teachers and thanked them. They didn't hear anything more from her that day.

When they came to work the next day, there was an email from Elizabeth's office. Jane's eyes welled up in tears and Lou was furious! The email read: "Here are some of the errors I found in the handbook. I was quite surprised that there was a mistake on practically every page! Please review the handbook carefully and edit it before we get these copied." There were indeed errors on office forms contained in the appendices but no errors on any of the pages Jane and Lou had updated and edited. The book looked better, the information was updated, and the pages that pertained to faculty and staff were clean.

The teachers told Elizabeth how pleased they were with the new version. Elizabeth thanked them for their compliments, never mentioning the work Lou and Jane had done, and then she thanked the clerk who had typed the error-strewn forms in the appendices for making sure the handbook was distributed. Jane and Lou just shook their heads in amazement.

For the remainder of the year they continued to teach and do their jobs as department chairs. Lou transferred to a new high school at the end of the year; Jane stayed. She did, however, resign as chair of the science department.

Reflective Questions

1. Describe the communication that took place.
2. What conclusions regarding communication can you draw from this incident?
3. What could Jane and Lou have done differently?
4. What could Elizabeth have done differently?
5. At what points and in what ways might the relationships have been rescued?
6. What would you recommend Elizabeth do now?

Our Analysis

Elizabeth was excited to be appointed as principal, but she missed an opportunity to meet the faculty and staff and tell them how excited she was as soon as she was appointed. Her desire to give the former principal an opportunity to finish his tenure there before she greeted the staff may have been interpreted as disinterest on her part. Her late arrival made the staff nervous because she wasn't there when decisions regarding the crucial beginning of school needed to be made. When she arrived and faced the handbook concern, she missed another opportunity to build relationships by communicating well with two influential teachers in her new school. If she had communicated verbally with appreciation for the work done, she might have gained some initial support from the two teachers. Their support could inform the budding opinions of other faculty and staff members to Elizabeth's advantage. Her choice to chastise them in an email allowed the slighted teachers to return to the perceived insults in the email again and again, reaffirming their feelings of unjust treatment and allowing them to share the written words with colleagues. The first faculty and staff meeting was another opportunity to put anxiety to rest by explaining realistic expectations for staff and letting them know how she would support them.

What Elizabeth did for the remainder of the school year is not discussed. She may have begun to recognize opportunities to nurture relationships within her school, the daily interactions when one word of kindness, written or spoken, could begin to change the perceptions of her. Lou's transfer to another school and Jane's resignation as department chair suggest that Elizabeth is still communicating a notion that she does not value the contributions of her faculty and staff. Without the skills to communicate her appreciation and support for her faculty and staff, she will struggle to develop and nurture a vision of success that all members of the school community can hold in common.

It's Your Turn

Now we invite you to think about a situation in your experience in which **Leadership Connector, Communication** seemed to be strong and/or one in which communication seemed to be ineffective. You may wish to record your thoughts in a journal. Writing can help you think in more detail and focus, revealing truths you have not seen before. Or you may wish to reflect on the situation with a trusted friend to ask you clarifying questions and to summarize what he or she hears you say. The following questions and statements may help you to focus your thinking.

1. Describe the situation you have selected in as much detail as you can.
2. Who was involved and what roles did they play? What role did you play?

3. What did you notice about the words the participants used? Their body language?
4. What beliefs did the participants seem to bring to the situation?
5. How was consensus achieved or thwarted?
6. What seemed to work well?
7. What could have been done differently to improve the outcome? In what ways were relationships built or destroyed?
8. Can broken relationships be rescued? If so, how? If not, why not?

Critical Points to Remember about *Leadership Connector, Communication*

- People must understand the leader's expectations, believe that the expectations are ethical, and trust that they can meet those expectations.
- Listening is more important than talking.
- The leader's body language and actions must verify his spoken or written message or the receiver is likely to misunderstand, distrust, or disbelieve the message.
- A quick quip or a hearty laugh is well worth cultivating to ease tensions.
- The leader can "frame" or adjust the spin on a situation to instill hope rather than create anxiety.
- Hunches have worth.
- The leader will be judged by writing skills.
- An issue considered for consensus must be important to the work the staff is doing as a group.

Chapter 2

Leadership Connector, Support

> Leadership offers an opportunity
> to make a difference in someone's life,
> no matter what the project.
> *Bill Owens*

We Are Important to One Another

Like communication, **Leadership Connector, Support** is transparent; you know when it is present and you know when it is lacking. Support is a basic need. Teachers, staff, students, parents, and administrators expect and want to be supported. Effective leaders know that no matter where people work, they value support. This basic need is of utmost importance and must be met for people to be successful.

Support comes in many shapes and forms. It might be financial, material, physical, emotional, human, and/or moral. When leaders demonstrate these various types of support, they are communicating that they value and care for their teachers. Support communicates connectedness. Support yields overwhelmingly positive results because it not only helps to build relationships, it also strengthens them. When we are supported, we experience feelings of belonging, we feel important and we feel relevant in another person's life. Support results in empowerment; it makes individuals feel on track and encourages them to keep on going. Support makes us feel good about ourselves and about the person or persons who are supporting us. Our need and desire to excel is heightened; we are much more likely to succeed if we are supported.

As leaders, let's think about how we feel when we are supported by faculty and staff, the assistant superintendent of curriculum and instruction, the superintendent and the board. In addition, let's think about how we feel when we have support from family, friends, children, neighbors, etc. These pleasant thoughts are ones that leaders want to evoke in their teachers; this is done by communicating effectively as described in the previous chapter on communication and by demonstrating support.

Teachers and staff look for the safety that support provides. When leaders provide support, they are saying, "You are important to me; you are important to our school. You are needed, wanted, and valued." Seyfarth (2001) emphasized that all individuals want to experience psychological success. Teachers want to come to work; they want to do a good job and will enjoy their jobs when they receive support. When the leader provides support, teachers and staff reciprocate. They watch out for, take care of, brag about, defend, and protect the leader. Support, however, must first come from the leader. Support begets support; it becomes mutual. It becomes something on which the leader too can rely.

It doesn't take very long for teachers and staff to determine if our second **Leadership Connector, Support**, is present or absent. If support from the leader is lacking, the road may become rather rocky. When support is lacking, the best and brightest will leave or they will band together to marshal the necessary resources to ultimately get rid of the leader. However, when support is present, teachers work in concert with the leader to develop a community of learners in which all are successful.

In this chapter we discuss Support. We examine what it really means in education to be supportive and supported. We discuss how support connects us to others and why support is critical in forming relationships. We begin by setting the stage.

Setting the Stage

It is gratifying to visit schools and find teachers who have a textbook for every student, supplemental materials that enhance the text, and the materials and supplies to effectively carry out the technical core of teaching and learning. We are also pleased when we enter classrooms that are spotless. Bulletin boards with pertinent information directly related to what the students are learning and Smartboards being utilized as diverse teaching and learning tools confirm our beliefs that teachers and leaders are working collectively to advance student achievement.

When classrooms are clean the school is usually clean, reflecting the importance of the school to the entire community. Many administrators tell us that they work hard to find the needed money in the budget to ensure a safe and clean environment in which teachers want to teach and students want to learn. Teachers in these successful schools are not spending substantial sums of their own money to buy materials and supplies that the district should supply; they are supported by their leaders.

Unfortunately in some other schools, teachers are spending their own money and these expenditures occur year in and year out; they are accepted. There are those who give up and make do with what the district provides because they realize that they will never be reimbursed for the money they have spent. This shouldn't be the norm in any school in the United States.

In order to raise test scores and increase student achievement, the leader must set the stage at the beginning of the year by providing what teachers need. As the year progresses it is necessary to replenish what is needed. By doing so the leader demonstrates his support for the teachers, students, parents, and the community.

Think about what it would be like if you were going in for major surgery and the surgeon did not have the scalpel he needed or the anesthesiologist had old equipment that worked only sometimes. Frightening, isn't it? We expect the surgeon and every one else at the hospital to have what they need. We should expect the same in every school across the nation. Student achievement depends on good teachers; to be good at what they do they need the leader's help. It is the leader's job to set the stage for academic success. Leaders might want to consider the following suggestions:

- Determine what is needed at the school site.
- Walk around, talk to teachers, visit classrooms, observe what is going on, and take inventory. Does every student have a book? Does every teacher have the equipment needed and does the equipment work? Does every teacher have a desk? Are their enough desks for the students? Are the classrooms clean? Are the custodians emptying the trash cans? Are the windows clean? Investigate personally and communicate personally. These might seem like rather pedestrian suggestions; however, the presence or lack of materials and supplies along with the condition of the school site communicates many things about the leader and the school.
- Start with little things first. Make a list of what is needed. What can be provided immediately? It may be as easy as providing pencils and paper or a kind word, or it may be as difficult as providing additional

teachers and staff, badly needed texts, computers, LCD projectors, Smartboards, or other equipment.

- If you have no idea where to start, contact the appropriate supervisor or a fellow administrator and ask for advice about how to acquire the major resources that are lacking.
- Examine the budget with a fine-tooth comb. Determine how much money there actually is in the budget. What funds are encumbered? How can categorical funds be best utilized?

The key is to first determine what is needed and then begin the process of getting it. One can't do it all in a day but one can have a beginning in a day.

A Cautionary Tale

Marilyn was hired for her expert knowledge in mathematics and her keen ability to teach and hold students' interest in math for an entire math period, day after day. The district and the school were fortunate to get her since she was recruited by many districts. She was notified in June that she had the position, and she was ecstatic. In mid-July she went into the school's office to ask questions and to get as much information she could about the upcoming year. The principal wasn't in so she talked to the administrative assistant. When Marilyn asked which classroom would be hers, she did not know. When she asked for a copy of the teacher's manuals for the classes she would be teaching, the administrative assistant indicated that they didn't have any, but she would order them.

Marilyn did not know what to think but kept plugging along. Two weeks before school started she was assigned a classroom. The following day she went to see her new room and started to get it ready. To her surprise the classroom was empty. She had expected desks for the students and a desk for herself. She went to the administrative assistant and asked for advice. She told Marilyn to go to the custodian, which she did. Three days later she had student desks. She had asked for a teacher's desk and was told that they were all gone and one would be ordered for her. They expected it would be in within the month. Without saying anything, she went home, got her desk out of her home office, and her husband and his buddy delivered it to her classroom. When school started some teachers wanted to know why Marilyn got such a beautiful desk. When Marilyn explained her story and told them that she had brought her desk in from home, they shook their heads.

About a month later, a gigantic box arrived and was placed outside her classroom. The administrative assistant explained that Marilyn's desk came in and that she had asked the custodian to assemble it. It took two weeks for that to happen. The desk was put together and left outside Marilyn's classroom on a day that the superintendent and some of his cabinet members were visiting. He stopped in and asked Marilyn why the desk was sitting outside her classroom. Marilyn innocently relayed the story to the superintendent. You can guess what happened next. The superintendent was furious and voiced his dissatisfaction when he spoke to the principal.

At the end of the year, Marilyn left the district and accepted a position in a nearby district. If the stage had been set and her basic teacher needs met throughout the year, she probably would not have left.

Desks should never cause such a problem for leaders or teachers. The need for basic supplies should be evident. The leader is responsible for having supplies and materials in each classroom when school starts. Asking teachers to provide a list of materials and supplies needed to facilitate their work demonstrates the leader's support. It will serve the leader and the teachers well if the leader solicits teachers' needs at the beginning of the academic year, midway through the year, and at the end of the year. This monitoring of needs heads off problems and allows teachers to teach instead of worrying about what they don't have. The leader may not be able to fill all the requests; nevertheless, communicating with teachers by asking for their input will display the leader's support and concern.

Effective leaders are as familiar with the school budget as the school administrative assistant or clerk. Knowing how much money is coming in, its origin, where it is going, and what must be encumbered will enable the leader to plan and purchase what is needed. Although a leader's day is hectic and roles of the leader seem nebulous and frenetic at times, we encourage leaders to take time, think about the budget, and reflect on the following questions:

- What are the roles and responsibilities of my position related to school budget management?
- Have I delineated these and shared them with my assistant principals, leadership team, office personnel and faculty?
- What is my step-by-step process for developing our school's budget?
- Who will I involve in the budget process?
- Who are our school's decision makers?
- What is my plan for monitoring the budget?
- Where can I get help if needed?

Reflection on these questions might spark some other questions, cause one to focus more on the budget, or be an affirmation of what the leader already knows.

Support in Action

Rose is an assistant principal who has a solid background in school finance. She shared the following school budget story with us. At a faculty meeting one of the more outspoken teachers asked the principal if she would share the budget with the entire faculty. The principal happily agreed to do so.

The principal returned to her office and asked the administrative assistant to prepare a small strip of paper for each teacher. The following is an example of one of the strips.

	Sept.	Oct.	Nov.	Dec.
Name ____________				
Copying	$22.00	$43.00	$66.00	$90.00
Paper	$18.00	$29.00	$30.00	$49.00
Staff Development		$293.00		

If the teacher had attended any staff development, the amount paid for him or her to attend was also on the strip. When all of the strips were prepared the principal shared them with the assistant principal. Rose had taken a number of finance courses in her administrative preparation program and really enjoyed working with budgets. Rose highly respected the principal and was concerned when she saw the strips; she did not want her to be embarrassed at the next faculty meeting. Rose gently asked the principal if she might add some information, and if she so desired, she would help her with the presentation of the budget. The principal was more than receptive; she admitted to Rose that she didn't know much about budgets and would take all the help she could get. It was clear that they had developed a relationship.

For the next week they worked on a strategy. The assistant principal did a lot of tutoring and the principal was extremely thankful. They planned a PowerPoint presentation on object codes, various fund sources, encumbered funds, categorical funds, and reserves. They presented this information to the faculty at the next meeting.

Their presentation met with resounding success. When they were done they asked the teachers if they could provide any further information. The teachers were so impressed that there was silence in the room. The outspoken teacher thanked them. Knowing the budget, sharing the budget, and being upfront with the teachers paid off for these two leaders as it will for you. Teachers at this school constantly brag about their "budget savvy" leaders! The moral of this story is:

- Know the budget inside out.
- Get help from another principal/assistant principal/colleague if needed.
- Manage and monitor the budget with the administrative assistant.
- Ask teachers/leadership team for input and share the budget with them.

We know an outstanding principal who sat down with her faculty at the beginning, middle, and end of the year. She presented the budget to them and discussed it line item by line item. She gave mini budget lessons in which she emphasized that 80 to 85% of every district's budget goes to salary and benefits. This helped the teachers understand why such a pittance is left in a budget for books, materials, supplies, and everything else. Teachers were constantly aware of how much money there was, where it came from, and where it was going. If they had a question, they would come into the office, ask the question, and walk away with the answer. If they asked a question in the hallway, faculty lounge, or faculty workroom and the principal didn't have the answer she told them she would get back to them, and she did. There simply weren't any secrets or hidden money. If money had to be set aside, justifiable reasons were given for doing so. You might want to think about these strategies and determine if any of them will work for you.

The following is another story about a knowledgeable principal. One December a number of teachers were complaining about not being able to make more copies on the school's copier. The principal shared the budget and the midyear copying costs with them. The teachers were aghast that so many thousands of dollars had been spent at this point in the school year for copying. They all agreed that they did not want to spend *their* money that way. Teachers actually started using the whiteboard, PowerPoint, and the overhead projector. They only ran the copies they needed, not the usual 15 or 20 extra. The secret was they collectively owned the budget.

Effective leaders use their school's budget to support teachers in increasing student achievement and enhancing the lives of their students. These leaders provide teachers with what they need to be successful. The end result is that teachers recognize and appreciate their support. They experience satisfaction in what they are doing and are encouraged to work even harder. This sense of purpose and fulfillment filters down to the students.

You Are My Most Important Asset

Even more heartening and rewarding than the material support is the emotional support leaders provide in some schools. Teachers long for this support. Effective leaders know that faculty and staff have personal lives. They may be raising children, caring for elderly parents, dealing with cancer or another illness, getting a divorce, getting married, buying a house, etc. Teachers cannot leave their personal baggage at the school door. That just isn't as easy as it sounds. Their personal lives are part of who they are. While a leader can't let teachers' personal lives overshadow and impact their jobs, their personal lives can't be ignored.

Leaders are not expected to be psychiatrists or full-time counselors; however, we encourage you to provide a supportive environment in which teachers will feel secure, safe, and comfortable enough to let you, the leader, know what is going on. Leaders must support everyone and must be aware of the damage that is done when some individuals are supported and others are not.

Years ago Barbara Streisand sang a song entitled "People." Although this is a rather dated song the words are powerful. In the lyrics are the words: "People, people who need people, are the luckiest people in the world." Even if you have never heard the song, we hope these words resonate because leaders need the people in their schools. Successful principals realize that it is virtually impossible to do the job alone; they realize that they need people. Margaret Wheatley (2004) reminds us that thinking a leader can do the job alone is simply nonsense.

Consider the pins and buttons that often appear in schools, in magazines, and at conferences that say "Children First." Why don't they say "Teachers First?" Here is the rationale for such a politically incorrect question. Teachers are the most important asset in schools. Yes, the students are the reason we are there, and we must serve our students, always do what is best for them, and support student-centered learning; however, teachers are the conduits to students. Teachers are in the middle between the leader and the students. The best way to increase student achievement is through the teachers. Mindful and enabling leaders recognize that they must support, recognize, value, respect, and celebrate the teachers in their schools. These leaders champion communication, support, trust, and safety with all teachers first in order to encourage and enable them to put children first. The leader should take the initiative and focus first on developing relationships. Once a cohesive unit is formed, together all constituencies can put "Children First." Perhaps, then, we might consider buttons that say "Teachers Matter," "Our Teachers Rock," "We Value our Teachers," or something similar.

As mentioned earlier, teachers are the most important asset in our schools, and as such, it is incumbent upon the leader to develop a healthy and collegial organizational school culture in which:

- Communication flows freely in all directions,
- Support is mutually provided,
- Teachers and staff feel physically and psychologically safe,
- Trust is deep rooted,
- All have and are able to demonstrate and utilize their competence, and
- Continuous renewal is modeled and practiced.

So, You Don't Like All of Them

Time and time again we hear, "I like the students but I can't stand the adults that I work with." These adults make or break a school; these adults will make, break, or ignore the leader. Equally important is the fact that these adults are the ones that have the knowledge, skills, and power to improve a school's test scores. So, it's paramount that leaders recognize the importance of the adults in their buildings. Doing so makes the road to increased student achievement a road that all want to travel versus an uphill, treacherous, and dangerous road that eventually goes nowhere.

Everyone can name people who annoy them or people they do not respect. It is normal to have different feelings toward different people; however, these feelings must not get in the way of one's leadership. In a school there may be individuals whom the leader doesn't like; nevertheless, as the leader, he must make the first effort to get along with them. Outstanding leaders demonstrate respect *first* even if some of the faculty don't look like them, act like them, dress like them, or think like them. Leaders are wise to demonstrate a willingness to work together *first* because they are role models for their faculty and staff. Teachers expect the leader to support them, all of them.

Teachers and support staff know if the leader values and respects them. A leader might say, "They don't respect me so why should I respect them?" Our simple answer is because you are the leader! The leader sets the tone, encourages or discourages, values or doesn't value the faculty, and determines whether or not he will do everything to ensure that all are working in a healthy versus toxic culture. There is something good in everyone. The leader may just need to dig a little deeper with some people to find that special something. If the leader decides from the very beginning that he does not like some people and then chooses to demonstrate this dislike, there is trouble on the horizon. Some people can be obnoxious, but the leader must find a way to work effectively with them.

It is not good practice for a leader to talk about teachers or other administrators. This demonstrates a lack of common sense and lack of knowledge. If a leader backstabs teachers to other teachers or administrators, the leader's reputation suffers. Effective leaders do not accuse because accusations are serious and do not demonstrate support. They refrain from talking to teachers and staff in an accusatory and demeaning manner. When people are accused of something, especially if they have not committed what another is alleging, it is very natural for them to become defensive and outraged. Effective leaders reflect, gather facts, and are willing to share these facts and names of individuals who have alleged that something has transpired. Effective leaders never accuse anyone of anything, rather they ask for help to better understand what has happened. More often than not, teachers will work together to clarify a situation if they are supported, valued, respected, and if the leader is sensitive to their feelings.

What Can I Get for You?

Visibility is influence. Exemplary leaders know that in order to be successful they must be visible. Spending the majority of the day, every day, out of the office, greeting teachers, listening, observing, talking with teachers and students, greeting parents, talking with custodians, taking coffee out to the bus drivers, troubleshooting, supporting, and building trust will help build relationships. When one is visible, teachers, staff, and students are provided with a special sense of security. When leaders are visible, people are appreciative of their presence. Being visible sends a message that one cares about what is going on at the school and everyone in the school. Sure, leaders have many things to do, such as answering emails, returning calls, attending meetings, etc.; nevertheless, effective leaders center their days on being visible. Being out and about for the major part of the day with teachers, support staff, and students will ultimately benefit the leader. Very often being visible is a large part of the answer to major problems in our most challenging and troubled schools.

We know of numerous successful leaders who are constantly seen throughout the day, who are in touch with the teachers personally, know the names of all the students for whom they are responsible, and are visible in the community. These are the leaders who have garnered respect in their schools, their districts, and their communities.

Frequently administrators tell us that they can't leave their offices because they are too busy putting out fires or too busy disciplining students. When a leader is in the office all day disciplining students, it is apparent to all that the leader does not know how to deal with discipline. It lets them know that the leader might not know what works and what doesn't work related to discipline. One might say, "I have teachers that are always sending students to the office for minor things." If this is the case, the leader should spend more time walking through the school and visiting classes. If one has students in his office constantly, it is a good idea to get teachers and/or the leadership team together and ask for their help. As a group, seriously consider developing a discipline/consequence code that will work for all and one that will be followed by all. In an environment of fairness, dignity, respect, support, trust, and effective communication, teachers will work with the leader to solve problems.

In middle and high schools that excel, large numbers of students are not waiting outside the administrators' offices in anticipation of some punishment. In these outstanding schools, leaders are visible, not the students; students are in class learning. Leaders at these schools tell us that if the leader is out and about, sees and talks to students, teachers and staff, problems will decrease because the leader has the pulse. When the leader is visiting classes and observing what is going on, students and teachers are much less likely to cause problems. Teachers are more likely to be teaching and students are more likely to be learning because they sense that the leader might be right around the corner; they expect to see the leader and are less likely to engage in negative behaviors. Visiting classes is also a great time to reinforce all of the wonderful things that the teachers and the students are doing. Walking around the school is a great time to let the custodians know how pleased the leader is with the cleanliness of the school. This is a great time to let staff know how appreciative the leader is of what they are doing. The key is being cognizant of what everyone is or is not doing.

A good practice is to walk around the school with the head custodian and together determine what needs to be done. This has to be done only a few times a year, and before one knows it custodians are walking around themselves making notes and prioritizing what needs to be done. Like teachers, they require materials and supplies. Like teachers, the leader must communicate with, support, recognize, value, and celebrate the support staff. Each and every one of their successes should be highlighted.

A principal we know has a head custodian by the name of Leroy. In his school there are four other custodians that work with Leroy. Each week the principal selects a day and over the public address system compliments Leroy and his staff. He asks teachers, students, and other support staff to thank them when they see clean floors, clean windows, clean bathrooms, or whatever it might be that was particularly clean that week. This celebration of a custodian and his staff encourages them to work harder and to focus on another area the following week because the principal will highlight them again. This unique principal does the same for the cafeteria staff, clerical staff, bus drivers, and of course, the teachers. This principal establishes his leadership and credibility by being supportive and cultivating relationships.

The following story is about a young leader and what he did to promote a sense of support and security in his school. Tyler, a new assistant principal, decided that when he assumed his new position at the middle school, he was going to be very visible. This particular middle school was known throughout the district for its discipline problems. When Tyler arrived at the school each morning, he walked around outside and inside. He talked to students before and after school, stopped by each teacher's classroom to say hello, talked to the custodian and cafeteria workers and made sure they had coffee. He walked the halls during the morning and then spent time in his office doing paperwork, answering emails, and returning calls for the rest of the morning. At noon he walked the entire campus again; he spoke to students, teachers, and staff. He never ate lunch alone. He ate in the teachers' lounge, the custodian's room, or in the lunchroom with the students. For an hour after lunch he walked the halls again and returned to his office. When students were dismissed, he was out of his office once again. He made sure he was outside; he observed the kids getting on the buses and then proceeded to visit teachers and wish them a pleasant evening.

At first the teachers, students, and staff didn't know what to think. Some thought he was nuts, some naïve, and others thought he was checking up on them. His visibility seemed somewhat over the top. To their surprise, they began to notice that discipline problems were sharply decreasing, teachers that had a tendency to slack off were working harder, and those who were doing a good job would invite him to their classrooms to show him what they were doing. When he was out to a meeting, or in an IEP meeting, or for some other reason not out and about, students and teachers would ask where he was. Teachers weren't constantly sending kids to his office for discipline because as he walked through the school he was able to put out fires.

Furthermore, he was able to get teachers what they needed because he either saw what they needed, or they told him. He had the pulse of the school and everyone in it. It seemed that everyone wanted to please him. He was developing trust, communicating, demonstrating what he expected, providing support, and building relationships. He was visible, a consistent role model and, as a result, there were great dividends. He was communicating the school's core values, he recognized those who worked hard to serve the students, and he did a superb job of identifying and celebrating the heroes and heroines in the school.

Word spread throughout the entire district that discipline had improved, his suspension numbers decreased, and that he was doing a great job because he did not stay in his office all day. Tyler was a role model not only for the school but for the entire district. He was able to focus on teaching and learning rather than discipline.

Being visible communicates something about the leader as does staying in the office all day. Credibility is built by being visible. Once a leader has established credibility, teachers and staff are much more likely to follow. Leaders have much more influence when they are visible.

Let's Not Eat Our Young

Schools are interesting places. Although schools are densely populated, adults who work there are isolated from one another. We liken schools to big boxes within which are a number of small boxes. Each small box, figuratively speaking, in the big box represents a room with some boxes slightly larger than the others. Each person or a small group of people, for example the cafeteria staff, gets a box. Each day people go into their boxes. Teachers go into their boxes, custodians in their box, and administrators in theirs. In many schools, thank goodness not all, individuals stay in their boxes for most of the day. Teachers come out of their boxes to go to their mailboxes, to pick up their students from lunch and recess, and then they come out of their boxes to go home. You know the drill and can probably visualize it as you read this.

New teachers are surprised by this isolation especially because they are at a developmental stage where they want and need contact and intimacy with others. They want to belong; they want friends and colleagues, and, more importantly, they want to know that there is someone at the school who will guide, support, and protect them.

The first year of teaching is a critical year for the new teacher, the students, and the school. A lack of experience in the classroom coupled with being thrust into a new isolated environment without the protection, assistance, and guidance of the university supervisor and the cooperating master teacher may result in the surfacing of insurmountable problems and stress for the new teacher. Teacher preparation coursework, fieldwork, and student teaching provide a panoramic view of what teaching is all about; nevertheless, student teachers really do not experience the full essence of teaching until they are thrust into their first teaching experience. For many the first year is catastrophic. They soon learn that isolation is expected and accepted and eventually they too will enter their boxes and will come out very few times during the day. How sad!

Frequently for our neophytes, isolation turns into desperation because they come to realize that there isn't someone to talk to or someone to turn to without the fear of being judged incompetent. Some make it; unfortunately many do not. Effective leaders set as one of their first priorities the eradication of this isolation phenomenon, not only for beginning teachers but all teachers. This is done by being visible, communicating with and supporting teachers. Isolation is eradicated when teachers see the leader, when time and energy are dedicated to inducting and mentoring them, and when time is scheduled each day for teachers to talk and collaborate with one another.

Eradicating isolation can be time consuming, yet the benefits derived are well worth the time the leader devotes to the task. Leaders who want to focus on this topic might consider monthly breakfast meetings to celebrate birthdays, holidays, faculty accomplishments, or anything else that highlights faculty and staff. Consider asking faculty to share one great thing that happened to them since last month at the next faculty meeting. Initially, teachers might think this is silly, but as the months pass they will be thankful that the leader focused on the good things in their lives. Teaching at times can be very challenging. Consider distributing monthly index cards (index cards should also be available throughout the month). On these cards teachers and support staff are asked to list the things that aren't going well, and, more importantly, they are asked to identify what the school as a team could do and/or what the leader could do to help. The goal is to get them actively involved in the solution. They might begin by writing concerns ranging from leaky faucets, to irate parents, to students not doing homework. Sometimes they might just want to moan, groan, or vent, and that is okay, too. They appreciate being listened to. They appreciate being part of the solution.

Let's Take Care of Them

A leader's display of benevolence toward teachers will be reciprocated. As the leader nurtures the growth of self-efficacy in others, his own increases as well. This reciprocity encourages a "can do" sense of purpose across the school culture.

New teachers, especially during the first two weeks of school, often seem like kindergartners who are so happy to go to school for the first time. New teachers beam from head to toe, their eyes glisten, their rooms are prepared, their grade books have the names of their students written in alphabetical order; they are so excited to begin their careers as teachers. They are hoping to see the leader's eyes glistening, also. They are hoping that the leader is excited about them. In March, for many, not all, the glistening in their eyes is gone. The glow they had that very first day is gone, and they have lost their enthusiasm because their classrooms are fraught with discipline problems. They begin to wonder if they have chosen the right career. Many will leave during the first or second year.

Successful leaders insure that beginning teachers are inducted. They take an active role in their development even if the district offers a support and mentoring program for beginning teachers. In order to initiate the induction process, we offer leaders the following suggestions.

Begin the year preferably in August with at least two breakfast or luncheon meetings with beginning teachers. These meetings should be voluntary. Be sure to have regularly scheduled meetings with them throughout the year for the purposes of inducting and mentoring.

At the first meeting in August, do the introductory kind of things:

- Introduce yourself, introduce your new teachers, introduce them to their mentors,
- Let them know what they can expect from you and what you expect from them,
- Take them on a tour of the school and their classrooms,
- Introduce them to everyone you come in contact with that day,
- Go over the students' handbook and the teachers' handbook,
- Give them their class lists, and
- Give them the keys to their rooms. Make a big ceremony of doing so. Remember, for many, this new job as a teacher is a dream come true.

Before they leave ask them to write down a list of questions they have on large index cards and collect them. Tell them that you will have the answers to all of their questions the next time you meet together. Emphasize that no question is dumb. Remind them that you too were a beginning teacher, and you know how they feel.

When the first meeting is over, force yourself to sit down and reflect. What went perfectly, and what will you do differently next time? This journaling will not only help you at your next meeting, it will help you next year when you have your first meeting with your new beginning teachers. When your first meeting is over, read their questions and formulate answers. Many of the questions will be very basic and others may require some thought. It's important that you reflect and formulate answers as soon as possible after that first meeting.

Have your second meeting about a week later. At this meeting, focus on their questions and focus on classroom management. Ask some of your outstanding veteran teachers to come in and talk about how they handle discipline problems. Allow for questions and answers. Give them a few short vignettes and have them work in groups of four to discuss how they would handle the problem described in the vignette. Then, with your veteran teachers, tell them what you would do. Be sure not to put your new teachers on the spot because they may not know what to do and may feel embarrassed if called upon. Review your discipline code and assure them that you will help them with classroom management. Make sure that you have identified a mentor for each teacher who can help. Please make sure that the mentor wants to be a mentor, not because they want the stipend, but because they are willing to help a new teacher grow. The match between the mentor and the new teacher has to be a good one; chemistry is important; it has to be right and time must be provided for them to meet on a regular basis.

Throughout the year hold bimonthly meetings to address various topics and issues. The key is that you get them together, listen to them, and support them. The very first time you dread a meeting, ask yourself why, reflect on what is going wrong, identify the resources you need, and go about the process of securing the resources. The time you spend on your new teachers now will pay off in the future. If you are visible, if you induct them properly, match them with a good mentor, guide, protect, and support them, they will become the excellent teachers they aspire to be. The payoffs of induction and mentoring are incredible.

You Make Me Feel Important

Kelly, a dynamic principal in a nearby district, does an excellent job of inducting new teachers. Once they are hired, she sends each new teacher a personal note congratulating the teacher on being hired. Approximately a week later, she sends them a packet with all of the necessary materials pertaining to the school and district. Next, she sends them a letter inviting them to come in and meet her. When they do so, she takes them on a tour of the school and introduces them to everyone present on campus. She gives them the keys to their new classroom and invites them to come in and work in their classrooms if they would like to. When the school year begins, she introduces the new teachers and asks veteran teachers to volunteer to help them. Because she inducted these veterans when they began their careers, they readily volunteer to help. Meetings are held on a regular basis with the new teachers and their mentors. Very seldom, do new teachers leave her building. Over the past ten years, the time and effort expended on these new teachers has surely paid great dividends. The relationships in this school are phenomenal. Kelly has succeeded in developing a culture of caring and helping.

What Did the Teacher Have to Say?

Support is protection. Teachers need the leader's support when they run into situations with irate parents and irate community members. It is a slippery slope when parents call complaining about a teacher especially since parents want an immediate answer. Sometimes they just want their kids to quit complaining, but other times they are justified in their complaints, and something has to be done. At the same time the leader must proceed with caution and engage in serious reflection on the matter because the leader does not want to destroy precious relationships that she has developed and nurtured over time.

If a parent alleges that a teacher or employee has done something serious and/or illegal, common sense tells us that the leader must act immediately. If, on the other hand, the parent is complaining about homework, or something that may have occurred in the classroom, or the playground, etc., then it is always best to ask the following question, "What did the teacher have to say when you spoke to her?" Nine times out of ten, the parent has not spoken to the teacher; therefore, it is wise to tell the parent to make an appointment with the teacher, discuss the problem, and together develop a solution. When the leader has finished the call with the parent, it is prudent to alert the teacher that the parent called, tell the teacher what was said, and let the teacher know that you are available to sit in on the meeting if the teacher needs support. Effective leaders provide protection. Effective leaders also make a point of sitting in meetings with parents and teachers if the teachers are new. Effective leaders let the teacher run the meeting and inform parents that they are not permitted to yell or use profanity if they start to do so. Effective leaders make it clear it that they are there to support the teacher and the parent; collectively they can solve the problem.

Conversations with the Reader

A Walk on the Bright Side

Now it's your turn. Read the following story, and reflect on the ways effective **Leadership Connector, Support** is demonstrated. See the questions at the end of this story to guide your reflection.

Mary

Mary was hired as the principal of Highview Middle School in June. She was thrilled; her dream had come true. She called Tony, the principal, who was retiring and asked if she could meet with him and perhaps have a tour of the building. She also asked if it would be possible to meet the support staff and any teachers that might be available when she visited. Tony invited Mary to the school the following Monday and Tuesday. This was a good time to come since teachers were there finishing up the school year and the students' last day of school was Friday. Tony was great! He met with Mary for two entire days. She met everyone and was assured by Tony that she would love her principalship.

Mary left Highview very happy and proud to be the next principal. During the summer, Mary spent at least two days per week at the school with the exception of two weeks when she went to Spain on vacation. During the summer she analyzed the school's budget, checked on the purchase orders, checked class rosters and class size, and made sure the building was spotless. She also talked with the teachers that came in and constantly asked if they needed anything. She noticed that teachers started coming in more often, she had many more conversations, and she really learned about the school's organizational culture. A group of the teachers invited her to lunch. Mary was thrilled; meeting for lunch was a great way to build positive relationships.

She sent a letter out to all of the teachers telling them how excited she was to be selected as their principal. She wrote a little about herself, her family, and her dog, Gigi. She wrote about what they could expect of her and clearly discussed what she expected of them. She received cards thanking her for the letter. Some of the teachers pledged to do their best; some were amazed that she sent the letter since they had never received a friendly letter outlining what would be expected of them and what they could expect of their principal.

When Mary returned from Spain, she began preparing welcome back boxes for the teachers. Inside each box were pencils, pens, staples, tape, markers from the school supply closet, and a number of school items she got on sale at Target, Wal-Mart, Office Max, Staples, etc., over the summer. In each box she also put a nice but inexpensive memento from Spain. She knew the back-to-school boxes might be viewed as goofy or silly; however, she remembered clearly what it was like, especially her first year as a teacher. She had to scrounge around for everything; she didn't know who to ask and ended up buying what she needed herself. She continued to do so until she became principal. She didn't want any of the teachers at Highview to ever have to worry about supplies. She wrapped all 72 boxes beautifully and wrote each teacher a personal card which was attached to the box. In the note cards she included some of the things she and the teachers talked about over the summer; the goal was to personalize each message. Her goal was to begin the year communicating, demonstrating support, and demonstrating that she cared about them.

During her first year things went swimmingly. She and the teachers collectively developed a discipline policy. All students and parents were informed. Mary, the teachers, and the support staff agreed to stick together and support one another in implementing and reinforcing policy. Teachers agreed to help the new teachers with discipline. They checked on the new teachers and mentored them. Mary went in at 6:30 each morning to check and respond to emails. She was visible throughout the day as was the assistant principal. The new discipline policy cut discipline problems by 90%. Her motto was "In unity there is strength."

They had monthly breakfast meetings at which each teacher was asked to share one thing that was going well. They were also asked to share one thing that wasn't going well; teachers were then asked to reflect on these and come to the next faculty meeting the following week with solutions. The support staff also attended these breakfast meetings. Often things that were brought to the forefront were easy to take care of, e.g., garbage cans not being emptied, a few of the same students being tardy, students not doing their homework. These turned out to be easy because custodians would say, "Don't worry. We'll take care of it," or teachers would say, "I can help you with the tardy problem, and I know how to help with the homework problems." Emergency types of situations were never brought to the breakfast meetings because teachers knew they could go to Mary immediately if they had a serious problem and together they would find a solution or Mary would know whom to call.

That first year Mary, the teachers, and support staff worked hard and became one of the first schools in the district to form a school business partnership with the largest insurance group in the city. The partners were active in the school. They came at 3:00 to tutor students, they came on their lunch hours to work individually with students, and they were visible in the cafeteria, on the playground, in the library, and at extracurricular activities. They had fundraisers at the insurance company to raise money for field trips and to purchase library books for each classroom. They had the sixth, seventh, and eighth graders spend a day at the insurance company. Each student had an employee to shadow throughout the day. One year the insurance company was remodeling and decided to give the school as much used furniture as the school wanted. Each teacher got a desk, a leather chair, tables, computer tables, and filing cabinets. Sure, they were used, but they were so much nicer than the ones they had!

The partnership with the insurance company and all of the monetary, material, and human support they provided would have never happened if it had not been for Mary, but she never let anyone know it. She never took the credit. She always praised her teachers and staff; she highlighted and bragged about them constantly. According to Mary, it was they not she who made the school run smoothly, and it was they not she who raised the achievement scores year after year. As one would expect, the teachers tell it another way and constantly brag about "Our Mary."

Mary is still the principal at that middle school; she has been there for 25 years and the teachers and staff continue to respect, trust, and love her. She still gives the welcome back boxes each year; however, the interesting caveat is that now the teachers look for things on sale at Target and various stores to put in the boxes. They also prepare a super special box for Mary not only at the beginning of the year but at holiday time, on bosses' day, on her birthday, and at the end of the year. This end of the year box is called the "See You in September Box."

Reflective Questions

1. How would you describe Mary's approach to supporting the teachers and staff at Highview Middle School?
2. Do you think the support in this story is by accident or by design? Explain.
3. What worked? What did she do that could transfer to your situation?
4. What surprised you in this story? What puzzled you? What would you do differently?
5. How do you think Mary supports students, parents, and members of the community?

6. If you had a chance to speak to Mary, what would you say or ask?
7. How were relationships built?

Our Analysis

Mary was young when she became principal; nevertheless, she recognized how important it was to learn about the school's organizational culture. She also recognized how important it was to learn from the retiring principal. She made the effort to contact him first to ask if it would be possible to meet with him. This allowed her to get to know about the current principal and the school, and this opened the door for her to meet faculty and support staff.

Mary knew that visibility was the key to developing relationships. When she toured the school with Tony, she had the opportunity to begin developing relationships with everyone she met. She was able to observe how individuals interacted with other individuals. In addition, she spent at least two days per week at the school during the summer at which time she had an opportunity to get to more acquainted with everyone at the school.

Mary was a master of communication. In addition to talking with teachers and support staff, accepting the teachers' invitations to lunch, and being visible to help and listen during the summer, she sent out a letter telling all how excited she was to be their principal. She gave them background about herself. However, more importantly, she explained what would be expected of them and what they could expect of her.

Mary set the stage for the year by carefully reviewing the school's budget, checking on purchase orders, and making sure the building was super clean when the teachers and students formally returned. She remembered what it was like when she was a teacher, begging for supplies and spending inordinate sums of money on supplies that the district should have provided. As a means of further communicating, supporting, and developing relationships she was smart to prepare the welcome back boxes for teachers. She was even smarter to include a personal note in each box.

Mary was skilled at bringing people together. Once she had garnered the respect of her faculty, staff, and students, she reached out to the community and in concert with faculty and staff formed a school business partnership with a large insurance company. The partner provided human as well as financial resources that the school desperately needed.

Mary celebrated her faculty and support staff and made it a point to always give them credit for the school's accomplishments. The teachers reciprocated and gave her credit for all she had done.

It is clear that Mary assimilated into the culture, communicated constantly, and celebrated the teachers, support staff, and everyone else associated with the school. She demonstrated her competence, supported everyone, and provided an environment of trust in which all felt physically and emotionally safe.

A Walk on the Dark Side

Now read the next story and reflect on what went awry. See the questions at the end of this story to guide your reflection.

Ed

Ed had been trying for a number of years to get the teachers at his elementary school to keep current. In a sincere effort to be supportive, he would constantly put information in their boxes that described upcoming courses to be offered at the two nearby universities. He also put flyers in their boxes about conferences and district workshops. He had always set money aside in the budget for staff development.

Most of the teachers attended only workshops on in-service days when the entire district was required to do so. The vast majority of teachers didn't think they needed any coursework since most all had a master's degree. They did not want to leave their families for more than a day for a conference, and besides that, they were very happy with what they were doing in their classes. What they were doing had worked for them for the last couple of decades. Mrs. Hale, after all, had been using the same tree branches to demonstrate how to make a spider web at Halloween for the last 30 years. In fourth grade, Mrs. Neno still had the students make Popsicle stick figures for their play on colonial times; after all, her students had been doing this for 22 years, and, according to Mrs. Neno, they liked it. Mrs. Derotti still had the kindergarten children dancing the chicken dance at their graduation instead of demonstrating what they had learned. Life was fine for these teachers, and they saw no reason to change.

In December the school district implemented a new reading program. Ed was pleased! Teachers were required to attend reading in-services during the months of January, February, March, and April to learn about the new series. Ed's teachers attended the required in-services and most were less than enthusiastic about it. They agreed that the one they were using was just fine; besides, they were accustomed to it. One teacher remarked, "If it ain't broke, then why fix it." Ed knew that they would have to use the new series in September because it was mandated by the district; Ed thought there was hope.

When the new series arrived over the summer, Ed did what he had done when any new material arrived during the last two years. He opened all of the boxes, counted every item, and reconciled the number of items that came in with the purchase order. He had the custodians deliver the books to each classroom. As teachers came in during the summer, he told them that their books were in and encouraged them to take their manuals and whatever else they needed home to plan, if they so desired. Very few did; those that took them home were the first- and second-year teachers.

When the school year started, Ed included information about the new series in the welcome back newsletter. At the first Parent Teacher Association meeting, he invited a representative from each grade level to talk about the new reading series. During September and October some of the first and second year teachers embraced the new series and talked about the strides students were making. However, there was a large group that was not pleased with this change. Ed heard through the grapevine that these teachers were not using or fully using the books. So he decided to visit classrooms. He hadn't visited classrooms in a long time because the school was fraught with discipline problems. As he entered classrooms, some of the teachers would grab the manual and begin to act like they were using it, others would say they just finished reading, and others would boldly say that they didn't like it and wouldn't use it. Ed tried talking to these teachers; he met with each one privately, he met with them as a group, and he scheduled more in-services which some attended. Rather than write letters of reprimand or ask for guidance from the assistant superintendent for curriculum and instruction, Ed tried to work this out himself.

He tried to talk to each teacher again and was frustrated and angry, when Emily, one of the more senior teachers, came to him after school on a Friday afternoon. She walked into his office and said, "I have to talk to you. You need to stop bothering us. We're getting tired of your coercing us into using the series. If you don't stop, we are going to the union." Before Ed could say anything, Emily walked out and closed Ed's office door behind her. He didn't know what to do. He finished up what he was doing that Friday and went home for the weekend.

When he woke up on Saturday, he was furious. He decided that he would go to the school, go into the classroom of each teacher who was not using the new series, and toss all of the old series and the accompanying supplemental materials in the dumpster. It took him all Saturday morning to dump the teachers' materials; he went home feeling good that now they would have to use the new series. It so happened that the custodian, who usually emptied all of the cafeteria garbage, went home ill on Friday and came back on Saturday. He cleaned the cafeteria and then proceeded to dump the bags full of milk cartons, food the students didn't eat, messy/sticky food containers from the cafeteria, etc., right on top of the materials that Ed had dumped. This made it virtually impossible to retrieve anything in the dumpster because everything was covered in garbage.

Monday came, and off went Ed to the monthly principals' meeting. Ed told his close principal buddy what he had done on Saturday and his buddy replied, "Are you nuts? Are you sure you wanted to do that?" The assistant superintendent then called the meeting to order and said it was going to be a long one.

Meanwhile, at the school the teachers were in an uproar. They came in and found that things were missing from their rooms. They didn't know if someone had stolen their things; they wanted to know where their books and materials were. Emily, who had talked to Ed on Friday, was particularly infuriated. She was determined to find out what had happened and asked the teacher next door to keep an eye on her classroom.

Emily was on a mission. She went from classroom to classroom to find out how many teachers were missing books; she had a pad and pen and made a list of each teacher and what was missing. She went to the office staff to see if they knew where the books and materials were. They had no idea what had happened to them and wondered if they should call the police. She then went to the custodian's office, and Joe happened to be there. He said he was in on Saturday, and Ed was there tossing books in the dumpster. She went to the dumpster with Joe, and there they were. Frantically she tried to retrieve some of the books, but, since they had been in the dumpster since Saturday, they were covered with garbage. She managed to retrieve a few books, and then the refuse truck came, and away went everything.

Emily was wild at this point. She called the union president. She also called the assistant superintendent of curriculum and instruction's office and the superintendent's office and neither was in. The assistant superintendent was in the meeting with the principals, and the superintendent was meeting with the Chamber of Commerce. Emily requested to be given five minutes to speak at the board meeting the next day. Frustrated that Ed, the assistant superintendent, and the superintendent were all in meetings, she called two board members she knew. Emily also called the newspaper!

After the principals' meeting Ed went to lunch with his fellow principals. When he returned at 1:30, the assistant superintendent and the superintendent were waiting for him. Both were furious. The superintendent began the conversation with, "Ed, you know I don't like surprises. What the hell is going on? Board members are very upset, and the newspaper is calling every five minutes. I want an answer right now!"

Reflective Questions

1. What conclusions regarding support can you draw from this story?
2. What went wrong?
3. What could Ed have done differently?
4. What could Emily and the other teachers have done differently?
5. What would you say if you could talk to Ed and the teachers?
6. Were there any ways of rescuing the relationships?
7. How long do you think Ed will last as principal?

Our Analysis

Ed did not know how to provide the support faculty needed and didn't know how to effectuate change. People are not going to change unless they see a reason for change and unless they feel the change will benefit them. When it occurred to him that he lacked this knowledge, it would have been wise to ask for help from trusted colleagues. It appears that he didn't understand the school's organizational culture and more than likely did not fully understand the district's organizational culture.

Ed did not know what to do, so he kept doing what did not work over and over again. The relationship with Emily in particular appears rather sterile; ultimately, it became hostile. Communication and visibility are seriously lacking. Ed does not have the pulse of the school. Visiting classrooms on a regular basis and observing firsthand whether or not teachers were successful with the old reading series would have benefited him tremendously. The teachers in his school needed more support than flyers in their mailboxes.

Ed had reached his brink of endurance. He was not in control of his emotions and was infuriated when Emily came into his office that Friday. He didn't like being threatened and was going to get even, not realizing that dumping books and materials in the dumpster could end his career in the district. He acted on his emotions and was reactive, not proactive. He failed to take the time to reflect, reframe, and get the help he needed.

Ed did not communicate with his supervisors. He forgot the cardinal rule: Supervisors do not like surprises! Superintendents, in particular, do not like surprises! It would be almost impossible to explain and justify what was happening at this point.

It's Your Turn

Now, we invite you to think about a situation in your experience in which **Leadership Connector, Support** seemed to be strong or weak. You may wish to record your thoughts in a journal. Writing can help you think in more detail and focus, revealing truths you have not seen before. Or you may wish to reflect on the situation with a trusted friend to ask you clarifying questions and to summarize what he or she hears you say. The following questions and statements my help you to focus your thinking.

1. Describe the situation you have selected in as much detail as you can.
2. Who was involved and what roles did they play? What role did you play?
3. What beliefs and feelings did you bring to the situation?
4. What beliefs and feelings did the participants bring to the situation?
5. What did the participants need? What in particular did they need from you?
6. How were you able to help and support them? What seemed to work well?
7. What could have been done differently to improve the outcome? In what ways were relationships built or destroyed?
8. How can the broken relationships be rescued? If they can't be rescued, why not?

Critical Points to Remember about *Leadership Connector, Support*

- Support is a basic need.
- No matter where people work, they expect, want, and need support.
- Support comes in many shapes and forms. It might be financial, material, physical, emotional, human, and/or moral.
- Support yields overwhelmingly positive results because it not only helps us build relationships; it helps us strengthen relationships.
- Support results in empowerment; it makes us feel on track and encourages us to keep on going. When we are supported, we feel good about ourselves and the person or persons who are supporting us.
- Effective leaders need people. Effective leaders can't do the job alone.
- Induction and mentoring are critical. If the leader does not induct, guide, and support teachers, the union will.

Chapter 3

Leadership Connector, Safety

> The safety of the people shall be the highest law.
> *Marcus Tullius Cicero*

I've Got Your Back

Everyone needs to feel safe. Even the world's greatest daredevil makes sure that all of his equipment is in top shape before he soars across a raging river on his motorcycle. Unless he has a death wish, he and his team have searched out and minimized every obstacle before he jumps. His goal is to celebrate victory on the other side—not to crash and burn! As humans, we need to feel physically, emotionally, and psychologically safe to live our lives. We do our best work when our primitive instincts to fight or flee are calmed to a reasonable state. Only when we feel safe can we shift our energy from basic survival needs to complex thinking and reflecting.

We need our challenges and even occasional frustrations to keep our brains alive. Without them we wither. The key is to keep our challenges manageable. It is a state of heightened, anxiety-minimized attention that researchers Renate and Geoffrey Caine (2008) have labeled "relaxed alertness." Csikszentmihalyi (2004) has called a similar state, "being in the flow." Often we say we are "in the zone." All are attempts to describe the optimum intellectual and emotional place in which our productivity and creativity blossom.

When an artist closes the door of his studio, turns on his favorite music, melds with his paint palette, and forgets to come down for dinner, he is likely in a state of relaxed alertness, flow, or zone. When an ad writing team sits around a table in overstuffed chairs, brainstorms ideas for an innovative milk ad, and emerges hours later with a brilliant, new concept, the team members are experiencing relaxed alertness and operating in the flow or the zone. People thrive on complex problem solving when they feel safe. The fear and helplessness associated with threat fall away, clearing the path for creativity, productivity, and, ultimately, fulfillment.

Those who experience this relaxed alertness, flow, or "in-the-zoneness" report a heightened sense of joy and energy that leads them to seek the experience again. If a leader can orchestrate opportunities for people to feel this positive energy about their jobs, he is likely to create a positive school culture. Bullies and "jerks"—offensive titles based on offensive behaviors—can't survive in such a place. As the leader becomes more proficient with clear communication and providing support, his staff will feel safe enough to move into the creative/productive mode we describe here. Trust flows from competent action in these areas, and then within a climate of trust the leader can further develop his skills as a communicator and supporter. It's all reciprocal.

In this chapter we focus on **Leadership Connector, Safety**, the human need to feel safe physically, emotionally, psychologically, and intellectually.

We Must Minimize Our Fears

Violent threats and behavior in school have always frightened children and frustrated educators. From the bully punching a fragile child on the elementary school play yard to the bloody gang fights in the high school quad, violence breeds fear, frustration, and anguish. The world cried when Columbine, West Paducah, and Red Lake—small, rural communities that had never before made the news—staggered through a "new" type of traumatic experience, well- armed individuals slaughtering blameless people without mercy. That unthinkable, apparently senseless violence spread to close-knit university settings such as Virginia Tech, University of Illinois, and too many others to name. Educators can't be faulted for thinking twice about becoming leaders in a volatile climate where explanations for horrific actions remain inadequate. We feel vulnerable and outraged at the thought of it happening on our own campuses.

Although we will not fully explore the emerging research on school violence, we will comment on one of the most consistent findings: Perpetrators are often perceived by others and/or perceive themselves to be outcasts, alienated from the school community and the larger society in some way. They often report fearing for their own safety, being victims of bullies themselves, or feeling invisible and insignificant in the presence of others. In short, they haven't felt nurtured or included in *healthy* social relationships.

Such violent acts suggest that schools must become communities where caring, vigilant people create a culture in which *everyone* belongs—students, parents, teachers, support staff, and administrators. An often referenced story, *Cipher in the Snow*, by Jean Mizer (1982), described an incident in a small town in the mid-1960s in which a young boy stepped off the school bus and dropped dead in the snow. On investigation no one knew anything about him. Only a few knew his name. The principal struggled to encourage people to attend his funeral. Even his teachers didn't know him beyond the fact that he was quiet and daydreamed in class. Speculation had it that the boy died of loneliness and exclusion. He just didn't belong.

How easy is it for the same thing to happen to a student in today's schools, or to a quiet, dependable teacher, or to an efficient but isolated night custodian? We believe that it can happen wherever there are groups of people who have not developed a sense of responsibility and caring for each other. People in such school cultures don't feel connected to one another. Colleagues and students come and go, doing or not doing their work, but seldom or never reaching that productive state of flow and accomplishment together.

On the other hand, in some school cultures people are overlooked or ignored on purpose. This cruel behavior suggests a bully may be at work, shattering the hope for a culture where relaxed alertness prevails. In this section we define bullying broadly to mean any intentionally hurtful behavior directed toward a target person(s) who is often less powerful than the bully. Using this definition, bullying can be covert as in the case of Joe or overt as in the case of Gerald, whose cases follow. It can appear anywhere and anytime as the examples illustrate.

Joe asked his two assistant principals to represent him at a recruitment fair in the eastern part of the country. Joe's district in California was having a difficult time recruiting teachers and decided to go out of state. His two assistant principals were ecstatic about recruiting new teachers. They prepared flyers, posters, a PowerPoint slide presentation, and a CD to distribute, and off they went to recruit teachers. They met with resounding success. Not only did they find enough qualified teachers for their school, they found enough for the entire district! The superintendent and the board couldn't believe it nor could the assistant superintendent of personnel. At the next board meeting, Joe was commended for what *he* had accomplished; he never recognized the two assistant principals for accomplishing this feat. At the next principals' meeting Joe was commended once again with no mention of the two assistant principals. Joe took all the credit. At the end of the school year, both assistant principals requested transfers to other schools. They realized Joe was notorious for taking credit for the good things other people did, and he was quick to blame others when things didn't go well.

Sometimes the bullying is more overt and aggressive. Skills learned on the school playground persist into adulthood unless the bully is stopped along the way. Consider this example from the larger society:

John plays poker regularly and enjoys the dynamics between players. He likes the challenge of figuring out if his competitors have better cards than he does and of betting skillfully, even pulling off a good bluff on occasion. He appreciates the banter as well as the silence, but mostly he appreciates play that respects the players and the dealers. He believes you must master the rules and the nuances of the game, but you also need to accept the role of luck. He often finds himself "in the zone."

One day Big Gerald arrived at the casino with a fist full of $100 bills. He bought a stack of chips that dwarfed the stacks in front of the other players and sat back with a smirk, daring the others to take his chips away. Gerald jabbered through every hand, rashly raising the bet by $500 when $40 would have been appropriate. Gerald filled the room with his voice. He chastised the dealer for not paying enough attention to the cards and the waitress for not bringing his food fast enough. John watched with disgust, waiting. Finally, Gerald began to bet a certain hand heavily, boasting that he could not be beaten. John said nothing, indicating with a tiny scratch of his finger on the table that he was calling each bet. Gerald got louder and louder, sure that his hand beat all others at the table. When it came time to show the cards, Gerald tossed his queens and sixes on the table, smirking and standing to add emphasis to his glorious triumph. John waited until Gerald's pompous boasting slowed. Without comment he turned over his queens and tens. Big Gerald swore, turned, and stomped away.

Gerald is a poker bully. He intends to victimize other players every time he plays. He makes the game tense for everyone. Some, like John, wait to "get" him; some are just uncomfortable. He wears people out. It's not fun to play with him at the table. The risk of humiliation is great. When Gerald plays, the focus shifts from the subtle camaraderie of the game to surviving the bully. Even players like John, who are not easy victims, change their tactics to meet the threat. Some players simply give up and leave. Imagine a Gerald in your staff meetings!

Bully Behaviors

Bullies often act in identifiable ways. Consider the following list of possible bullying behaviors:

- Harsh or invalid criticism,
- Micromanaging,
- Unrealistic expectations and demands,
- Taking credit for someone else's accomplishments,
- Public humiliation,
- Lies and two-faced behavior,
- Physical, verbal, or nonverbal threats,
- Uninvited touching,
- Isolation or exclusion from the group,
- Any behaviors that assure that the bully can maintain his or her power by demeaning someone else.

Young girls are practicing their bullying behaviors when they decide to exclude a certain girl from their circle and to tell everyone else they shouldn't be her friends, either. The adult version is the teaching team that excludes a new teacher from the weekly lunch get-togethers.

Bullies are everywhere—in the media, in the workplace, on the playground—even in the finest schools. No matter who they are, the effects of their behavior are similar. When a bully is at work, creativity, enthusiasm, self-efficacy, and collegiality decline. Compliance, hesitation, self-doubt, and isolation rise. When these conditions exist, stress stands tall, and tempers grow short. The zone, flow, and relaxed alertness fall away, and victims struggle to survive. Safety has fled.

A bully can be anyone. Bullies are males; bullies are females. Many bullies are bosses who use their power tyrannically, but some bullies are colleagues. In schools a bully could be the superintendent, the principal, a teacher, a parent, a custodian, a librarian, or a student. Anyone can be a bully.

In the following sections we examine bullies from three different perspectives: when the supervisor is a bully; when the site leader is a bully; and when someone being supervised is a bully.

Your Supervisor as the Bully

The power that goes with their position creates opportunities for cruel supervisors to assert their personal power over others. Superintendents must answer to boards of education that have the power to hire or fire them. They are public figures who must gain supporters in order to achieve their goals. Competent superintendents value and appreciate their supporters; they nurture their supporters toward a common, ethical goal with integrity and purpose. Incompetent superintendents may bully people to become their supporters so they can maintain the appearance of competence. You will encounter both kinds of supervisors in your career. When as a site leader you experience heavy stress, anxiety about achieving the expectations placed on you, professional threats if you do not meet the expectations, inability to sleep or take time for fun, more illness than usual, etc., look carefully at your circumstances. You may have a bully supervising you.

When you are being bullied by a supervising administrator proceed with caution. First, gather evidence to confirm or dispel your suspicions. Assuming the supervisor is out to get you could just be your own anxiety seeping out. Stress can do that to you. Take your time, and ask yourself some key questions:

- Is my evidence based on my own observations or on hearsay from others?
- Is the criticism I am receiving justified?
- Is the criticism undermining my success at my school site?
- Am I encountering unreasonable expectations, possibly more demanding than those placed on others in similar positions?
- Am I singled out in public for humiliation? Do others seem to be taking up the cause against me to gain favor with the supervisor?

After you consider these questions, you may determine that the criticism is justified, and you may decide to make some changes in your own performance. If so, you may choose to meet with the supervisor and ask for guidance in making those changes.

On the other hand, you may confirm that you are the target of bullying. This is a much more serious situation because the bullying supervisor is often motivated by feelings of personal inadequacy. This supervisor sees a competent employee either as a threat to be removed or as a foil to make him or her appear more competent. Our recommendation here is to nurture as many positive relationships as possible in the workplace to use as references when you move to another position. Be sure your work is documented, and keep witnesses around you when the supervisor talks to you. Look diligently for another position, so you can make the change before the bully makes it for you. Our recommendation may seem drastic, but if you are not the person with the power, you are not likely to get the respect you seek. Prepare to move on.

You, the Leader, as the Bully

It's difficult to look within ourselves and acknowledge that we are not treating our colleagues with respect; we may, in fact, be bullying them. When do we cross the line from being firm and principled, an admirable quality, to being abusive? "Firm and principled" means that we have a universal ethical purpose that guides our every decision and behavior. We operate from a basis of integrity with concern for others and have low tolerance for anything or anyone that detracts from the ethical vision we seek to achieve. We know that the Leadership Connectors hold the keys to success for our whole school community.

We cross the line when our fears about our own competence drive us to ignore our compassion for others and focus us instead on our own public image and our need for power. If our behavior is not directed toward a universal ethical goal, we need to examine what we are doing. For example, if you feel the need to establish yourself as the leader when you first arrive by bossing everyone around and finding fault with others, check your motives. You might be a bully-in-training covering your feelings of inadequacy.

When you fear you might be a bully, ask yourself the following questions. Be as honest as you can be. Your ability to reflect on and take responsibility for your own actions will make you a more compassionate and effective leader.

- Are my employees afraid to tell me when they make mistakes?
- Am I finding fault in others where fault doesn't exist?
- Do I feel threatened by a successful, competent teacher?
- Is there someone I exclude from meetings or conversations? Who and why?
- Has my staff become defensive or apologetic regarding their actions?
- Do people avoid me?
- Do I doubt my competence as a leader?

Sometimes your own stress and feelings of inadequacy can lead you to treat others unkindly. Be aware of your triggers, and be careful not to make others suffer for your negative view of yourself. Take time to become self-aware and to seek clarity in a situation so you can lead your staff toward achieving a common vision. In the story that follows, we see that Mitzi dug a hole that continued to deepen as one bullying episode led to another. Be cautious!

Mitzi was a third-year principal in a small high school. Most teachers had given up on her, simply avoiding her as they went about their daily work. Very few teachers were willing to help her anymore. She had taken credit for work done by others, made decisions without consulting people who were affected, screamed at teachers in staff meetings, and on and on it went. The brightest and best teachers had already left or were making plans to leave.

Mitzi had one teacher left who was willing to help. This teacher, Desiree, loved the school and the students, so she stayed. As science department chair she played a major role in writing the new biology curriculum. At a department meeting in November, Mitzi usurped Desiree's role as chair and ran the meeting herself. Teachers in the department had questions about the new curriculum, and they had concerns about the equipment that had not been funded for the new curriculum. Desiree had voiced these concerns numerous times to Mitzi who indicated that the budget didn't allow for the purchases this year.

Desiree decided to discuss the equipment issue during the department meeting because Mitzi hadn't responded to her private requests. When she did, Mitzi pointed her finger at Desiree and yelled, "Don't you talk!" Desiree was humiliated and outraged. She yelled at Mitzi and stormed out of the room, embarrassing herself by losing control. After that meeting, Desiree found excuses to be away from interactions with Mitzi and resigned at the end of the year. Mitzi is still at the school, achievement scores are still low, and the impression in the community is that nobody cares about what goes on at that high school.

We believe that Mitzi can salvage this situation if she is willing to self-reflect and begin to show her compassion and respect for colleagues. It will be hard, humbling work. If she is able to demonstrate these "high-road" behaviors, we think she will eventually find them to be automatic, and the responses from her colleagues will change toward her. We are confident that she will shine as a leader if she provides an environment where safety, trust, and support flourish. If you see yourself in any part of Mitzi's sad story, keep reading about the Leadership Connectors and think about what you can change before you reach this point with your colleagues.

You as the Supervisor of a Bully

You may have an administrative assistant who provides extra supplies to her favorite teachers and denies basic supplies to those she doesn't like or a history department chair who assigns coveted Advanced Placement classes to her treasured colleagues and remedial world history to the beginning teacher. You might also have a cafeteria supervisor who chastises and benches children and forces them to sit without talking through lunchtime. All of these are examples of bullying behavior, and they lead to fear, self-doubt, and stress in those who are being targeted. When others join the bully, condone the abuse, and/or ignore the behaviors, a toxic culture develops in the school. And toxic cultures squelch progress.

When a leader detects a bully working within his staff, it is not wise to ignore the behavior. The bully will require monitoring. Just as a leader has little power to combat a bullying supervisor, staff has little power to combat bullying by a more powerful colleague. A competent, ethical employee may be surprised to be targeted; in fact this person may not even realize that bullying is in progress until her reputation is tarnished. On the other hand, a weak, insecure employee may be too frightened to do anything about the abuse and may even believe that she deserves it. In either case, the bully will be enlisting others in his cause, eroding the positive opinions of others about the victim with lies and innuendoes. The bully manipulates the facts using partial truths and timing as weapons to place the target in a defensive position.

A leader may be tempted to demand that the bully and the victim "talk it out" and end their feud or talk it out in front of the leader. At that point the leader has fallen into a trap. The bully is more practiced at distortion of reality than the target is, making the target's protests sound hollow.

Toxicity creeps into a school one bully at a time, and the leader needs to find ways to weed them out or to avoid hiring them in the first place. The teachers and staff count on the leader to keep the workplace safe for them, so it is important for the leader to let them know that he will not tolerate bullying behaviors. Respect for everyone must be a non-negotiable rule for the school culture. Action on the rule must follow any infraction. That said, you might ask how to handle the occasional drift we all make into bullying behavior. Consider the following story for some insight into that question:

Karen had been teaching for 20 years and had recently been elected as president of the 800-member teachers' union. She was well known and well respected by teachers and administrators alike. Karen and her principal, Mario, had a strong professional and collegial relationship.

One afternoon Karen walked into Mario's office and exclaimed, "I'm in trouble! I just smacked a student's arm." Karen knew that Mario would be upset, but she knew that she could turn to him. Mario told her that she had to apologize to the parent and the student. He directed Karen to call the parent and ask her to come in as soon as possible to explain what had just happened.

The parent came in that same day. Karen explained that Jason, the student, had been fooling around all day, and at around 1:30 she had reprimanded him for the 100th time. He sassed her back, she lost control, and she smacked him on the arm. With tears in her eyes, she apologized over and over again and asked the parent and student to forgive her. Mario and Karen both indicated that she had done this out of frustration, and that she was wrong. Fortunately for Karen and Mario, the parent accepted the apologies and agreed that Jason had provoked Karen to act as she did. When the parent left, both Karen and Mario sighed their relief. Then Mario said, "Karen, you are really lucky this worked out this way. Your career could have been ruined. Don't ever touch a student again. If you do, you need to know that I will not support you."

Karen never did such a foolish thing again. When she retired 15 years later, she talked about how much she appreciated Mario's support, consistency, and predictability. Karen shifted the focus of her retirement celebration to the principal she knew she could trust—the person who made her feel safe enough to admit even an uncomfortable mistake and grow from the experience.

One bullying behavior does not a bully make! Mercy is an appropriate action in some situations, but a leader needs to act on every event in an appropriate way to be sure that one event does not become a pattern. The goal is to eradicate all bullying behavior, and the staff needs to know that.

There are several actions a leader can take to build a school culture free of bullying. For example, asking staff to complete anonymous surveys about how they *feel* working in the school can provide some base level information about the school culture. Then the leader can follow up with individual and small group discussions and ask staff to reflect on their own behaviors. A leader might spend staff meeting time identifying teacher expectations for student behavior and then move to discussing how staff members model or do not model those behaviors themselves. Are they modeling what they expect students to do? How can they show students what they expect?

If this approach doesn't stop the bullying, the leader will need to counsel the bully directly and privately, begin documentation and an assistance plan, and work with the human resources office to find the best solution. If left unchecked, bullying on campus destroys feelings of safety and belonging.

Consistency Matters

The school bus arrives at 8:42 a.m. The first bell rings at 8:52 a.m. Teachers and yard supervisors hustle students into classrooms. The final bell signals the start of the school day at 8:58 a.m. Teachers expect students to be in their seats ready to learn at 9:00 a.m. A student council member reads the daily bulletin over the intercom system at 9:02 a.m. Teachers report attendance via email, and class begins.

School days are filled with routines and procedures designed to assure orderliness and consistency. Orderliness frees the mind to concentrate on learning instead of reinventing ways to accomplish repetitive tasks daily. It brings a sense of security and unity, a common understanding of "the way we do things around here." Teachers expect orderliness. It helps everyone to know how he or she fits into the organization. Everyone needs to belong, and routines and procedures can provide the structure for everyone to find his or her place in the organization.

Like a climbing wall, these routines and procedures comprise the supportive structure that allows a common vision to emerge and to grow. The wall provides footholds for those who are climbing and harnesses to catch those who misstep. The climbing equipment is adjustable to fit the specific requirements of each climber. This flexibility allows each climber to reach the top.

Like the climbing equipment, school routines and procedures must be flexible and adjustable. Just as the needs of the climbers dictate the design of the climbing gear, it is the vision, the goal, the work that needs to be accomplished that determines the design of the routines and procedures in the school. When routines and procedures no longer support teachers teaching and students learning, they need to be revised.

Routines and procedures must be flexible but not capricious or arbitrary. They should be consistent but provide for unique circumstances when necessary. For example, a class rule that late work will *never* be accepted does not allow for a family emergency that prevents a conscientious student from accomplishing the work on time.

"No tolerance" policies are examples of inflexible procedures. In the name of consistency school boards often adopt no tolerance policies to demonstrate to the community and to potential offenders that the district is tough on crime and violence. These policies require that all students who violate the same rule be given the same punishment and that some offenses will not be tolerated even once, regardless of circumstances that may surround the violation. The site administrator of such policies must administer justice. Mercy is not an option. So what happens if a leader believes that mercy is appropriate in a given situation, but the policy prohibits mercy?

Carson's experience addresses this situation. Carson was a new high school principal when he discovered a serious drawback to a no-tolerance policy. A group of students had threatened to tromp another group of students, and the campus was on high alert for weapons. Parents had expressed their fear of violence breaking out on campus at the last school board meeting, and Carson was determined to protect his students from harm. One October day, campus monitors began patrolling the parking lots, checking parked cars for evidence of weapons. They found four knives and one revolver. The student drivers of the cars in which the weapons were discovered were members of the threatening group. Carson started expulsion proceedings in accordance with the board's no-tolerance-for-weapons policy. He was thankful to have such a definitive policy to squelch the violence before anyone was hurt.

The same afternoon the campus monitors discovered a butcher knife in the back seat of another student's car. They also found some newspapers and a plastic grocery bag with pumpkin seeds inside. Carson discovered that the student had driven the car to the YMCA the evening before and used the kitchen knife to carve Halloween pumpkins with a children's group. The boy had forgotten the knife was in the car when he got up late in the morning and rushed to get to his first class on time.

The policy was no-tolerance. It did not allow for extenuating circumstances of any kind. The boy would be liable for the same consequences as the other students who were intending to use the weapons violently. Carson explained the situation to the superintendent, and together they worked with the board to achieve a more equitable outcome than expulsion for the pumpkin-carving student. Ultimately the board revised the "no-tolerance" policy to give administrators more discretion to consider circumstances surrounding an offense.

This example demonstrates the importance of developing reasonable, flexible—yet consistent—policies, procedures, and routines. A leader cannot dictate policy, but he needs to be aware of ultra-restrictive policies that he is required to enforce. Think about various scenarios like the one Carson faced that would force a leader to enforce unjust consequences. Bringing those situations to the superintendent's attention could allow him to head off a bad situation.

We need to find a "place in the middle" where teaching and learning can take place in any situation. Often a busy leader attempts to streamline discipline in order to get on with more important concerns. She clarifies the offense, issues the punishment, and moves on to the next case. It's all very efficient, but we argue that it is not very effective. Discipline offers a prime opportunity for teaching. If we move directly from the infraction to the punishment, we skip over the "place in the middle" where mediation, reflection, teaching, and learning can occur. It is between the infraction and the consequence that one can help a student to define the problem clearly, reflect on his actions, identify alternative actions, and commit to what he will do next time. This seems fairly straightforward.

Now consider the same strategy used with teachers and staff. We all feel safer when we feel valued. When a leader is in the evaluator role as an administrator, he can easily fall into a practice of moving hastily from the situation (observation) to the consequence (evaluation). He may even decide to send comments out in writing without a chance for discussion. Generally, union contracts frown on such a practice, but it happens anyway, particularly when the leader is overwhelmed by completing numerous evaluations on a short timeline. We recommend that a leader take the time to discuss what he has observed with the teacher or support person before finalizing the evaluation. It takes more time, but it builds a sense of orderliness, respect, and consistency in the employee that promotes feelings of safety and gives the evaluator a clearer understanding of what he has observed.

Surprises Aren't Fun

A famous caution for all new principals is, "Make sure you tell the superintendent about anything happening at your school that may land in his lap. He doesn't like surprises!" Some superintendents ask for weekly "What's Cooking" type reports on issues that might affect the board of education or that might be discussed in the community. A wise administrator keeps a daily journal of these events and situations and faithfully reports them. It calms the superintendent's anxiety about being blindsided without a response. Additionally, keeping the superintendent informed about the good things happening at your school helps to build relationships between your school, the superintendent, and the board. It allows him to brag about what's happening in the schools.

An administrator represents the superintendent and the board of education to the community and may on occasion commit a faux pas. In a healthy culture, a leader can rectify such mistakes, as the following incident illustrates.

One of Sally's extra duties as principal of an elementary school was to chair a meeting for parents on the district's new reading program. The meeting was scheduled for the same evening as a board of education meeting in a conference room near the board room. Sally was setting up for the workshop when a parent came in. This parent had been asked to provide refreshments for the board of education meeting that night and asked Sally where to take them. Sally thought they were for her meeting. She thanked the parent and went on with her preparations for the workshop.

Sally's meeting went well, but the next day while she was cleaning up, she happened to hear her disgruntled superintendent berating another principal who was responsible for providing refreshments for the board meeting the evening before. It seemed that the refreshments had never arrived, and some of the board members had counted on them to replace their dinner. Sally was mortified, but she knew she had to fess up. She explained her mistake to the superintendent with heartfelt apologies and no excuses. She then wrote a letter of apology to the board members. Sally was ultimately forgiven, and the story became part of district lore.

Now put yourself in the place of a brand new teacher. This neophyte *knows* that she will make mistakes. She lives in fear that she will make a royal one. To avoid this possibility, she prepares and prepares, trying desperately to ward off what she perceives to be the inevitable. She can't possibly know everything that is and is not acceptable in the school culture until she has been there for awhile. She doesn't like surprises any more than the superintendent does, and you can put her at ease by simply giving her the most complete information you can about expectations, putting her in the care of a supportive team, and forgiving her missteps while she is learning.

If a leader plans ahead, he can prevent situations like the following:

Janene was a first-year teacher who had done her student teaching in a well-staffed middle school with multiple administrative assistants. It was the practice for teachers to give documents they needed to have typed to an administrative assistant who would do the typing and make as many copies as the teacher requested. When Janene arrived at her first official job, she came prepared with several documents to have typed and copied. The administrative assistant berated her for being such a prima donna, and Janene was humiliated. Fortunately, the principal, Jerry, overheard the conversation and followed Janene to her room. He listened to her explanation, understood her concern, and asked her what she needed. Then he told her Sally's story about the refreshments (see above), and they laughed together. Janene figured out how she could get her typing and copying done—nothing was urgent—and went on about her day reassured that it was an OK place to be. Jerry spoke to the administrative assistant, explaining Janene's previous experience and calling on her compassion. Then he made sure that information on typing and copying procedures was included in the packet of new teacher information for the next year.

And can this reaction to surprise affect the seasoned teacher as well? Just ask Joe. He was the well-respected Science Department Chair in his high school when the assistant principal of instruction suddenly died in the middle of the school year. Joe had an administrative credential, but he wasn't sure he wanted to leave teaching to use it. Joe's principal approached him to act as an interim AP and asked him if he had any interest in applying for the permanent position. Joe explained his reservations about changing positions and made an appointment with the principal to discuss the details of the changes that would be involved. In the meantime Joe agreed to fill the interim slot, and the principal announced his appointment to the staff. Joe received kudos from his colleagues and prepared to turn his classes over to someone else for the remainder of the year. He developed his list of issues to discuss with the principal about his decision to make the change permanent. Two days later, following the board of education meeting, a trusted colleague who had attended the meeting told Joe that someone else had been appointed to be the permanent AP. Joe gathered his thoughts and calmed his emotions. No one had told him about the new person. He was embarrassed and unprepared to face his colleagues. At the end of the school year, Joe left the high school, unable to come to terms with such a devastating surprise.

Or just ask soft-spoken Melinda who had taught French in her middle school for six years. One late spring day her principal, Karen, distributed the fall class schedule at the faculty meeting. Melinda's name wasn't on it. When Melinda asked about what she thought might be a missing page or a slipup in the typing, Karen snapped back, "Oh, I forgot all about you." With one thoughtless, surprise statement, Karen conveyed to Melinda that she did not value her presence. Melinda became watchful and cautious.

We can foster feelings of safety simply by being diligent—avoiding uncomfortable surprises for people and rectifying situations in which they were surprised.

It's 2:00 a.m. and My Heart Is Racing

When you find yourself watching the digital clock on your nightstand change to 2:14 a.m., and your body is telling you that sleep is not in the plan, your thoughts are likely trapped in a negative place. We rarely lie awake thinking about the delicious new ice cream flavor we had for dinner or the satisfying ending to the bestseller we just finished. In fact, illness seems worse at night, and mothers warn their teenagers that no good can come from activities that happen after midnight. Troubling thoughts about real or imagined situations creep up on us and refuse to let us go when we are tired and unable to will them away. This late night anxiety is a common affliction for harried school leaders. Over the years we have gathered several suggestions for getting the rest you need in order to maintain your health and to shine as the example of hope for your colleagues. If you are anxious, your whole staff will sense it and begin to be anxious as well. Their anxiety increases yours—and so it goes. Here are some thoughts taken from those who have slept through the nights as school leaders:

- *Practice compartmentalizing.* That is, learn to leave school at school. Your work will never be finished. As soon as you empty your "in" box (if you ever do), it will begin to fill up again. You must learn to walk away from it when it's time to go home. One leader made it a practice to arrive at school an hour before staff arrived and to leave two hours after staff left for the day. Although this made a long day, it allowed her to complete paper work in solitude, and it relieved her from taking it home. She knew how long her day would routinely be, and she saved her home to interact with her family. She left school at school and enjoyed home at home.
- *Prioritize.* You have a better chance of compartmentalizing successfully if you learn to do the urgent things first, the important things next, and the extra things if you have any time left. One administrator set up three drawers in his desk—one for what he must attend to immediately, one for things to complete over a period of time, and one to increase his general knowledge and to explore new ideas. Two advantages of this system are (1) the limited space in each drawer forced him to prioritize and to toss things out that stayed too long in the drawer, and (2) the drawer could be closed so he wasn't overwhelmed by huge piles on his desk.
- *Make a list of things you do to relax.* If your list is short, do your best to lengthen it as you hear others talk about what they do to relax, as you read books on the topic, or as you simply think of new ways to calm yourself. Others have turned to such practices as reading for pleasure, talking with a friend, exercising, listening to favorite music, going to a movie or sports event, attending a club meeting of friends with similar interests, going for a drive in the country, playing with children or grandchildren, working on a hobby, or whatever. Too often we feel guilty when we take these breaks. In reality, we are allowing ourselves to enter the workplace renewed and revitalized the next day. We can be much more productive when we step away from problems for a while and return to them with a fresh look.
- *Make a practice of listing all of the things that go well each day.* Type A, deeply committed leaders are so good at listing all of the things that are broken, they often ignore the great things that are working. We need to celebrate the good things! One group of administrators

began a retreat with everyone telling about something that had gone well at their schools during the past year. One told about a struggling student that he had mentored, another told about her teachers and staff embracing a teacher who was dying of cancer, one told about a new reading program that boosted the skills of several students in danger of failing, and on it went. At the end of the sharing, the room was silent, everyone filled with tender memories. With this prelude, leaders set the tone for their day. A focus on what is working instead of what needs to be fixed energizes people to think about how they can do more of what works. When we focus on problems, we see what is wrong; when we focus on successes, we see what is right.

- *Develop a support network of colleagues, family, and friends.* You cannot do this job alone! Surround yourself with people you trust.

Just as the other members of your school community need to feel safe there, the leader does, too. When the leader feels safe coming to school, others will, too. We will discuss these critical points more in depth in Chapter 5 when we think about Continuous Renewal.

Conversations with the Reader

A Walk on the Bright Side

Now it's your turn. Read the following story, and reflect on the ways **Leadership Connector, Safety** is demonstrated. See the questions at the end of this story to guide your reflection.

Marisa

The kindergarten team at Frost Elementary School had been together for many years. They loved their students and had their routine set so that they really didn't have to think about it or prepare for each day. Then the school demographics shifted. More poor, immigrant children enrolled who needed assistance. First grade teachers began to complain that children were not coming to them from kindergarten as prepared as they had in the past.

Marisa had been principal at Frost for two years and recognized that the four teachers on the kindergarten team were in trouble. Sarah, the team leader, and Heather, Sarah's partner teacher, had been successful with their students in the past, but there were many more children from poor families now, and the two teachers were struggling with the new group of students, many of whom did not speak English. Susan had once been a strong teacher, but now did just enough to get herself out the door on time at the end of the day. Marisa suspected Susan was burning out. Gladys, Susan's partner teacher, was close to retirement and focused on painting and cute projects.

Marisa followed a hunch and sent Susan to some advanced reading training in which she had expressed a slight interest. The training provided a conversion experience for her! Where she had begun arriving late, leaving early, and showing reluctance to try new things, she now beat everyone to the classroom, greeted her children with a big smile, and began to use a variety of new teaching strategies. She returned to the team ready to encourage big changes.

Gladys was willing to try some of the new strategies, but she couldn't muster the commitment it would take to make such major shifts when she was so close to retiring. Heather was interested but hesitant. She listened to Susan's suggestions, tried some, questioned some, discussed them with Susan again and then tried some again. Her interest started to build.

Sarah on the other hand rejected Susan's suggestions, proclaiming that she was already quite successful with her teaching. Sarah belittled Susan's teaching, pointing out that she, Sarah, was the senior member of the kindergarten team. Sarah then began to shun Susan in the staff room, inviting others to lunch and excluding Susan. She advised parents that they should not place their children in Susan's class because she was too rigid. She dropped hints to other teachers that Susan was really becoming overbearing and bossy. She neglected to tell Susan when team meetings were being held and then accused her of missing the meetings on purpose. Did Susan think she was too good for them? Then Susan's supply order did not appear, even though everyone else's arrived on time.

Susan became more and more stressed and finally went to Marisa in tears. She told her that she knew Sarah was sabotaging her, but she couldn't prove it. She had been so excited about the new strategies but was now questioning herself. Maybe she should just do what she had always done. Marisa reassured Susan that she was doing fine work and talked to her about how the change process works. She told her that change can be threatening to some until they feel safe and supported in trying something new and encouraged that they are capable of doing it.

Marisa monitored Sarah's behavior and had several conferences with her to identify her concerns. Marisa was able to calm Sarah's fears enough to see a change in behavior toward Susan. At the end of the year, Marisa assigned Sarah to third grade knowing that Sarah could excel with this group of teachers.

Susan's students' assessments showed that they were far more prepared to move on to first grade than students from the other three classes. First grade teachers asked Susan what she had done to get such results. Susan began to talk to them about the new methods, and they expressed interest in attending the training themselves.

Reflective Questions

1. How would you describe Marisa's approach to encouraging teachers to learn and use new methods? What worked?
2. What did she do that could transfer to your situation?
3. What surprised you in this scenario? What puzzled you?
4. What made you say "Aha"?
5. What would you do differently from Marisa? Why?
6. Do you think Marisa's staff feels safe working at her school? Why?

Our Analysis

Marisa had spent much time visiting kindergarten classes, looking at assessments, listening to interactions between kindergarten and first grade teachers, and observing the teaching assignments in the kindergarten team. She knew from the evidence she had gathered that the kindergarten team needed some type of change. She took advantage of an opportunity to send Susan to an advanced training workshop. Marisa weighed the evidence, pro and con, and decided that it was worth a try to challenge the status quo. When Susan returned so excited, Marisa watched for feelings of rivalry from the other teachers. Marisa wanted to be sure that Susan felt safe. She stayed close to the situation, knowing that any change can threaten people who may not feel confident about their own abilities to be successful with the change. When someone succeeds in changing "the way they have always done things around here," it can challenge the sense of security others feel.

Sarah was the team leader. She had the most power to lose, and if she felt inadequate to make a successful change, her fear could drive her to use her power to protect herself. Marisa watched for opportunities to provide Susan the support she needed without further antagonizing Sarah. Her goal was to make the level of anxiety that is natural to any change manageable for everyone. She wisely offered opportunities for the others to attend the workshops without holding Susan up as an example. Making Susan the poster child for new methods could have increased antagonism toward her. Instead, Marisa encouraged Susan to refine her skills within her own classroom, gaining confidence as she tried new ideas but not pushing them on others.

When the results were in, Marisa let others discover Susan's success. Marisa gained the confidence of other teachers because she supported Susan without flaunting her accomplishments and she was willing to stop the bullying behavior of a colleague without fanfare. In treating the situation this way Marisa let her staff know that it was safe to try new ideas and that everyone has a right to an emotionally safe place to work.

A Walk on the Dark Side

Now read the next story and reflect on what went awry. See the questions at the end of this story to guide your reflection.

Aida

Aida, a seasoned high school principal, had built up a strong following in her small, rural community. She knew all of "her kids" and their families well, often spending social time with them. Her small faculty loved her and the freedom she gave them to teach as they wished. They rose to her expectations to put "her" kids first. Students in her high school were successful because Aida was a loving "mother" to them. She was an icon in her community. Aida's approach was unconventional and individualized to each student's needs. She made an exceptional effort to meet everyone's needs with remarkable results. Most of Aida's kids came from low income and/or dysfunctional homes but they surpassed predictions with test scores, attendance rates, and college entry statistics.

Aida's reputation spread to the large district nearby. The superintendent called her and invited her to take over a large, struggling high school in his district. The test scores were far below expectations, the teachers were grumbling, and the 3,000 students seemed uninterested in learning. When Aida arrived, she stopped the lunchtime boredom with her playful and dynamic presence. Her sense of humor and outgoing style drew everyone to her. Students began to hang around Aida, even competing with each other for her attention. Teachers began to feel the electricity, the excitement of Aida's presence on campus. Hope returned.

Aida was caught up in her own success. These were good people. She was sure she could meet everyone's special needs as she had in her former district. For example:

- Joan's aging mother lived with her, and the caregiver had to leave each day by 3:00. School ended at 3:15, so Aida assigned Joan a last period conference to allow her to leave early, even though the contract specified that teachers must be on campus 30 minutes before and after school began and ended.

- John signed up for a cross-country bike ride that started two days before the school year ended, and he had used all of his off-work time. Aida told him to write a letter requesting special bereavement leave that she would sign even though bereavement was not the cause of John's absence.
- Aida's friend invited her to bring a few teachers for a holiday weekend at his beach condo. Aida took five teachers who loved to surf and play beach volleyball. They added a day to the already long weekend because the weather was so great. Everyone called in sick that day, and Aida approved it.
- Aida extended her favors to specific students as well. For example, Sammy was caught smoking on campus for the third time. The school counselor suspended him according to district discipline guidelines, but Aida responded to the pleas from Sammy's parents and reversed the suspension order. Aida socialized with Sammy's parents, and she knew that Sammy was a good kid. Sammy's friend, caught smoking with him, was suspended.
- Diana was a cute cheerleader, filled with personality, who missed six practices in a row and was benched by the advisor. Aida succumbed to Diana's tears and allowed her to cheer if she promised to attend practice from then on.

Teachers and students sought Aida's approval, competing with each other to earn it. Her approval was necessary for anyone to get perks, and the strong, vocal people got what they wanted. Others were denied benefits because Aida didn't have time for everyone. She would have liked to give everyone what they wanted, but it was not possible with 3,000 students and 250 staff members.

She was overwhelmed. The hope the staff felt when Aida arrived gave way to division—those whose needs had been met and those whose needs had been ignored. A counselor and an assistant principal resigned because they felt Aida was undermining their decisions. Student assessment scores remained low, and after two years, Aida moved on to another small district.

Reflective Questions

1. How is it possible for good intentions to result in increased anxiety?
2. What conclusions regarding emotional/psychological safety can you draw from this incident?

3. What could Aida have done differently?
4. What lessons, if any, do you think Aida took away from her experience at the large high school?
5. Were there any ways of rescuing the relationships?

Our Analysis

Aida gained the love and respect of students and staff in a small setting. She had a good heart and was able to see that people were treated equitably when she worked with their needs individually. In the larger setting she could not satisfy her need to be loved by everyone by giving special favors she had managed well in the smaller school. She could not be everyone's "mom." Her charisma, sense of humor, and good intentions could not make up for her inability to provide a consistent, ordered, and safe environment. The impossible number of personal interactions and favors it would have required to be everyone's hero actually caused more dissension because people began to compete for her attention and favors.

Flexibility must be built into routines and procedures, but the flexibility must lead to equitable not arbitrary outcomes. Aida's story demonstrates that too much flexibility leads to inequitable outcomes. People feel emotionally and psychologically safe in situations in which order is based on flexible consistency.

It's Your Turn

Now, we invite you to think about a situation in your experience in which **Leadership Connector, Safety** was present or seemed to be the issue. You may wish to record your thoughts in a journal. Writing can help you think in more detail and focus, revealing truths you have not seen before. Or you may wish to reflect on the situation with a trusted friend to ask you clarifying questions and to summarize what he or she hears you say. The following questions and statements may help you to focus your thinking.

1. Describe the situation in as much detail as you can.
2. Who was involved and what roles did they play?
3. What did you notice about the level of confidence with which the participants spoke and behaved?
4. What fears did the participants seem to bring to the situation?
5. How was a positive outcome achieved or thwarted?
6. What seemed to work well?
7. What could have been done differently to improve the outcome?

Critical Points to Remember about *Leadership Connector, Safety*

- Everyone needs to feel safe.
- As humans, we need to feel physically, emotionally, and psychologically safe to live our lives.
- Only when we feel safe can we shift our energy from basic survival needs to complex thinking and reflecting.
- Schools must be communities where caring, vigilant people make sure everyone belongs.
- Bullies can be anyone—your superior, you, or those you supervise.
- Toxicity creeps into a school one bully at a time, and it's up to the leader to weed the bullies out or to avoid hiring them in the first place.
- Routines and procedures are essential for peace of mind and must be both consistent and flexible.
- Having multiple ways to reduce your stress can keep you healthy and sane enough to do your job.

Chapter 4

Leadership Connector, Competence

> A competent leader can get efficient service from poor troops, while on the contrary an incapable leader can demoralize the best of troops.
> *General John J. Pershing*

We Know What We Are Doing

Some days you just don't feel smart. Maybe you thought you solved the discipline problem in Mrs. Hatch's room yesterday, and here it is again this morning, the same problem, with no apparent improvement; or maybe you studied the confusing, new format for your school budget, and you still have no idea how much money you have. Events like these trigger the beat-yourself-up days that send you home disputing your mother's advice that "you can do anything you set your mind to!" Obviously, your mother never anticipated events like these. You are certain that you do not have the skills, or even the potential, to do this job. In fact, you suspect you may be incompetent.

Let's pause this unproductive line of thinking and step away from education for a moment to consider Oscar's story. Oscar is not an educator, but sometimes recognizing that feelings of competence and incompetence are human and touch everyone's life path can bring perspective to our own lives. When thoughts and feelings of incompetence weigh a leader down, they signal a need to reflect and to reframe our experiences. And so we offer Oscar's story, likely a very different story from yours but one that can trigger insights if we allow ourselves to focus on the process, values, feelings, and aspirations Oscar exemplifies. His outlook on life can underlie success in every chosen profession.

Oscar graduated from high school and went directly to work for a small ready-mix concrete company in a low skill, stepping-stone job. Forty-six years later he retired from the same company, credited with building the company's reputation as the most respected in the industry. Though few competitors or customers would have recognized Oscar on the street, they all knew his name and his voice on the phone. He was simply "Oscar over at Rock Ready-Mix—call him if you want your concrete on time and mixed right." Quiet, competent, and diligent, Oscar worked in his computerized office—managing orders, dumping concrete ingredients into huge mixer trucks and dispatching the trucks to jobs, sometimes for 16–18 hours at a stretch. He was a legend in the industry.

As a young man, he did basic entry-level jobs—working in the gravel pit, moving material in a dump truck, and cleaning up the yard—but his employer soon recognized that he was a jewel worth polishing. Oscar watched, listened, and did his job well. He became an expert at pulling levers to mix complex formulas that varied by individual job requirements.

Well into his career, he began to hear about computer software that could simplify the mixing process. Oscar had no experience with technology. Like so many others from his generation, he didn't own a computer and had no idea how they worked. But he recognized the potential. He understood the vision, even when others didn't. He picked the brains of computer representatives and tried things out for himself. Soon the reps were coming to Oscar with problem-solving questions, and competitors called him for advice. Once again, Oscar became an expert as he had so many times before. He later said that pulling the levers required such physical endurance that he knew his body would eventually wear out. The computer assistance would make it possible for him to push buttons instead and to keep doing the job he loved. An added benefit was that he kept the company on the cutting edge, competing successfully with the "big guys."

Oscar was competent, and he knew that maintaining his competence would require effort. He knew that he needed to:

- Listen, observe, reflect, and analyze.
- Find a reliable, knowledgeable person to teach him what he couldn't figure out on his own.
- Expect to make mistakes and understand that they clarify the next steps to take.

- Embrace the changes that could improve his performance and increase company success, even if it meant giving up the way he had always done it before.
- Take the extra time and do the hard work it would take to develop his skills.

The result of living life this way brought Oscar respect from colleagues, customers, and subordinates. He earned their trust and was sought as a mentor.

Many educational leaders know what Oscar knew, too, but they may not yet have raised this knowledge to a conscious level. Without knowing and practicing these competence-building skills, a leader is inclined to wallow in the self pity that results from feeling inadequate or incompetent. In this chapter we discuss Leadership Connector, Competence, and we invite you to think about your own sense of competence and how you can reduce the number of those "I'm-a-total-idiot" days.

I Didn't Know That!

A leader must recognize that he will never know everything he needs to know. In this age of overwhelming amounts of information, only a supernatural being can be omniscient. There will always be more for a leader to learn. The good news is that there will always be a way for a leader to learn what he needs to know. The resources are there, not always in conventional places. It is up to the leader to find and use them.

When a leader doesn't know something important, he has at least two ways to respond: (1) Use "I didn't know that" as an excuse and walk away from the issue, or (2) learn what he needs to know and use the knowledge to address the issue in a productive way.

It's tempting to use "I didn't know that!" as an excuse when things go wrong. Sometimes a leader seeks ways to completely avoid a sticky situation, so he pleads ignorance. When a leader chooses to avoid, people soon catch on that the leader will run from a difficult situation. They learn they can't count on that leader to support them. Bullies take that as a sign to move forward with gusto while their targets retreat into fear. If a leader succumbs to the temptation to claim ignorance and walk away from a dicey issue, he often finds that the issue seems to fester and grow, becoming more painful as he continues to deny its existence. Yes, excuses are tempting, but they bring unhappy consequences far too often. We have something better to suggest—the competent way to respond.

Forget the "I Don't Know" Defense

"I don't know" doesn't have to be an excuse. We can all get inspiration from those who say, "I don't know—yet! But I will know soon." Being able to identify times when we don't know something important and then to know how to find the resources to gain understanding is an invaluable skill for a leader.

Remember Martin from the Communication chapter? He had never even taught in elementary school before he became an elementary principal. He learned on the job, just as Oscar, the ready-mix legend, did. Martin was wise enough to know that administrators become competent by paying attention to the world around them and the interactions of the people in it. Like Oscar, he listened, observed, reflected, analyzed, found mentors, made mistakes, spent the time it took to learn from the mistakes, and made the necessary changes. His reward was the respect and trust of his staff. They saw him as a dedicated learner who valued their expertise.

Martin framed his initial ignorance about elementary schools as a quest and began his journey toward competence. In a nutshell, he (a) clarified what he needed to know, (b) gathered the relevant information, (c) used the information to make sound decisions, (d) took appropriate action, and (e) moved on to the next challenge, more prepared to handle it. Sound like a simple formula?

If a leader frames "I didn't know that" as a catalyst for action rather than an excuse, people will join him in the quest at hand. Like Don Quixote, most people enjoy the challenge of a quest rather than the drudgery of "fixing" a problem. Building competence is a quest for better ways to reach a worthy vision, not a taxing interruption to the "real" work. Enjoy the journey to being able to say, "I can help you with that," instead of, "I don't know."

I Want to Feel Good about My Job and Me!

We all want to feel good about the job we are doing, but how do we accomplish that? These days we are often told to praise our children and honor all of their accomplishments, even when the accomplishments are small, so that our children will feel good about themselves. The claim goes that self-esteem, i.e., feeling good about one's self, is critical to happiness.

Others admonish, "Spare the rod and spoil the child! Excessive praise only creates a child who thinks he's better than he really is and who grows up expecting unending recognition for every move he makes." The argument rages, but perhaps these views are simply two sides of the same coin, each needing the other to produce a whole. We suggest another way to think about this issue. Let's consider an underlying concept that must be healthy and well nourished if positive self-esteem *and* a sense of a job well done are both to occur.

The key concept here is *self-efficacy*, i.e., a person's self-appraisal of how capable he or she is of accomplishing tasks and attaining goals. When we know that we have worked hard and achieved something of value and quality, we feel satisfied, sometimes even proud. And if this pattern of success continues, we confirm our beliefs that we are worthy people. We experience high self-esteem based on our competent actions. Our constant self-talk says, "I can do this—no problem," or even, "Bring on the next challenge!" When our self-talk confirms that we can do something, we are more likely to try to do it again or to increase the complexity of what we attempt.

But we know that everything we attempt will not be perfect. In fact, it is important to understand that our mistakes and failures bring us to the next step in competence. It is at the point where what we already know slips into what we do not yet know that the learning occurs. Reflection is at work at this point. The mistakes and missteps that we make are essential to our understanding and growth, and the reactions of others are crucial to how we view our stumbles. If our childhood mentors helped us to recognize that our mistakes were part of the learning process and required us to try again until we clarified the competent way to move forward, then we have probably learned to keep trying until we achieve the outcome that merits praise.

Our early mentors can encourage us to move forward without resorting to insincere praise. A mentor can be kind, yet clear, about what needs to be done differently, perhaps not with a rod, but rather with honesty and directness. In the words of a first grader, "I like my teacher, Mrs. Jackson. She doesn't yell at us; she just tells us what to do."

By the time a leader becomes a principal, she is fortunate if she has internalized the conversation that her lifetime mentors instilled in her to discriminate between completing a high quality job, and being in the learning stage, still making mistakes. In the learning stage, she is not yet an expert, but she knows she will get there if she just keeps reflecting on and analyzing her steps along the way and making adjustments when necessary.

On the other hand, when we believe that something is too hard or that we are incapable of doing it, we are less likely to try to do it. If our childhood mentors criticized our mistakes, and we failed to develop constant self-talk that told us mistakes are part of learning, we may give up when criticism comes our way. We may come to believe that making a mistake signals failure. None of us wants to fail, so we have no incentive to attempt the things we believe we can't do.

In the chapter on Safety, Sally made a mistake in assuming the food a parent brought was for her workshop rather than for the board of education meeting. Her self-talk told her that this was an uncomfortable part of her learning process—a mistake. Nevertheless, it was a learning opportunity. She apologized to the superintendent for her mistake, so she could move on. Her experience made her much more vigilant and conscious of her assumptions thereafter. Her ability to clarify a situation improved. She became a more competent leader as a result.

From Sally's example, one can see that self-efficacy is related to the notion of "framing" we discussed in Chapter 1. When we believe in ourselves and our capability to accomplish things, we behave in ways that will make our attempts achievable. For example, if I believe that I am capable of running ten miles, I will frame the task as a challenge that I can meet. I will prepare myself by buying practical, stylish running gear so I look like a runner, and then I will run short distances until I increase my endurance to complete the entire ten miles. I will do things that will make that challenge an opportunity to grow rather than an insurmountable problem. On the other hand, if I believe that my body is not capable of running ten miles, I will probably not make the attempt at all.

This self-belief that we are capable and doing everything we can to achieve what we set out to do creates a cycle of success. The belief leads to successful behaviors, and success confirms our belief and makes us feel good about ourselves. Feeling good about ourselves happens when we accomplish what we believe we can do and what we organize ourselves to achieve. It doesn't happen just because someone tells us we're great or beautiful or smart. Compliments may be something we are conditioned to expect from others, but unless they confirm our own perceptions that we are doing a good job, they can be quite hollow. It's what *we believe* about our own capabilities that determines how we *behave*.

So, as a leader you may go ahead and celebrate your staff members' accomplishments with ice cream rewards on Fridays, quick notes telling them they are phenomenal, and movie tickets when they reach their goals, but you must remember that underneath it all is the self-efficacy issue—do *they* believe they can accomplish certain goals, and can *they* make a plan to reach them? These beliefs about themselves are even more influential than their actual potential in determining their behavior. A person can be a potential math whiz, but if she doesn't believe that she is, she won't behave as one; or a person can have no obvious potential as a math whiz, but if she believes she has potential and she perseveres to achieve it, she just might surprise everyone.

Self-efficacy enhances motivation, productivity, high-quality work, and self-esteem; self- doubt kills them. In the children's story, *The Little Engine that Could* (1930), a tiny engine was tasked with moving a heavy load over high mountains. The little engine just kept saying to himself, "I think I can; I think I can" until he reached the top. It was hard work, but he was willing to tackle it because he believed that he had the potential to do it if he just put in enough effort. A leader needs to examine her own self-efficacy. Does she believe she can handle the job even though she may run into the occasional "I'm-so-stupid" day? And is she willing to put in the effort and forge through the mistakes to accomplish her goals?

What If I Feel Stupid All The Time?

Humans have the capacity to modify their self-efficacy beliefs. Even as adults who had poor childhood mentors, we can strengthen or weaken our beliefs about what we are capable of doing in the following ways:

- *Our interpretation of the experiences we have.* If we believe we have succeeded in an endeavor, we affirm our self-efficacy, and we try something similar or more challenging in the future with confidence. If we do not believe we have succeeded, even if other people believe we have, we are less likely to engage in the action again.

  We all need to hold thoughts of times when we glowed with success. A leader can make a list of experiences in which he overcame incredible odds or drew on something deep inside him to change an outcome for good. Then he has those experiences handy to lean on when his current situation stumps him.
- *Our interpretation of what we see others do.* If we see good models of the action we are asked to take, and we believe our capabilities are similar to the model's, we are likely to try what the model does. If we cannot identify with the model, we may decide not to engage.

  This suggests that a leader should cultivate relationships with people he admires and respects, observe how they handle a variety of situations, and apply what he learns to his own situation. Conversely, a leader should avoid negative people.
- *Our interpretation of the encouragement other people give us.* If we believe that the encouragement we receive is genuine and that the results are attainable, we are likely to try something new. But there is a caution here—we are more likely to be influenced by the negative judgments of others than their positive encouragement.

If a leader develops supportive networks in which she encourages others, and they encourage her in return, perhaps she will offset the negative comments she encounters along the way. She should choose to be in the company of supportive people as much as possible—friends, mentors, family, etc.—and never hesitate to call someone she trusts to ask for encouragement and reassurance when she needs it.

- *Our feelings—emotional and physical—about an activity.* If we have positive "gut" feelings or emotions associated with the activity, we are more likely to engage in it. If we feel stressed or frightened by it, we are less likely to engage.

  Here it may be best for a leader to acknowledge his negative feelings, recognize that fear or anger will control his feelings about attempting something if he lets them, and then push through the bad feelings and make the attempt. For instance, if the leader speaks to a PTA group and falls flat on his face, he should acknowledge it, think about how he can improve, try it again, and create a new experience for himself while gaining the admiration of the group for persevering.

If a leader knows these attributes of developing efficacy, he can analyze his own self-talk to see if he is falling into any traps. Likewise, he can try to identify the obstacles his staff may be creating for themselves in their self-talk.

Now let's focus on how a leader's feelings of competence may have changed when her title moved from "teacher" to "administrator." When she began teaching, she probably had a curriculum to follow, maybe some textbooks, perhaps some course outlines or syllabi. If she was lucky, she had a department chair, grade-level leader, or administrator who could tell her what she was expected to teach and provide her with a handbook. Then she began to organize her own classroom, setting expectations, and developing routines and procedures to make things run smoothly for the students who came to her every day. She increased her competence by taking university courses in her subject area or teaching methodology, asking the teacher next door for help and materials, and maybe even observing another teacher. She didn't quit her job after the first year, so she must have developed some degree of success in the classroom. As an administrator, everything changed for her with respect to orderliness, routines, and procedures.

One administrator we know took all the classes necessary to earn administrative certification and then said to a colleague, "But what can I expect a day to look like? What should I *do* on the first day?" The more experienced colleague laughed and said, "Don't worry. It will come to you!" Gaining competence as a leader is not as clear-cut as gaining competence as a teacher.

There are no lesson plans. Coursework is necessary, but painfully incomplete. A leader learns on the job, refining as she goes. Every situation offers its own unique opportunity for finding resources and developing expertise.

A Cautionary Tale

Naïveté or fear can sometimes lead a new or incompetent administrator to sabotage his faculty's and staff's opinions about his competence as you will see in the story of Nathaniel. Nathaniel was a new, 26-year-old assistant principal attending his first faculty meeting as an administrator. The principal introduced him and asked him to say a few words. Nathaniel jumped up and stood proudly in front of 72 high school teachers and 30 support staff. He was well dressed, had a new haircut, and exuded enthusiasm. He looked so young. He began by saying, "I have been in this business for a long time, and let me tell you what I expect of you based on my many years of experience." He continued by delineating his expectations. The teachers and staff couldn't believe their ears. Some of them were old enough to be his parents and some his grandparents. There he was talking about his four or five years of experience as a teacher (none as an administrator) and his extensive knowledge base. The vast majority of teachers tuned him out and did so for the rest of the year. His career as an administrator was short and fraught with problems. He went back to teaching. We would like to think that in a few years he actually acquired the vast experience he claimed and returned to administration.

No one expects a leader to know everything even though questions may come to her on every imaginable topic. A leader can learn to say, "I'll find out and get back to you," when she doesn't know the answer. A leader's competence will speak for itself. No need to tell people that she knows what she is doing.

What Do I Really Need to Know and How Can I Learn It?

We've thought about the skills and knowledge one really must cultivate to be a successful leader, and we offer the following list. It seems to us that a leader will not survive long in administration if he doesn't master these skills. You may wish to use the list as a reflective tool.

- *Social/emotional intelligence.* If you were a successful teacher and if you have been hired as an administrator, chances are good that you have at least basic skills in this area. If you are a quiet listener, you will need to develop your assertive, decisive skills; if you are assertive and decisive, you will need to develop your quiet, listening skills. Successful administration requires you to listen with care *and* to act with conviction.

To hone these skills, observe, observe, observe; nurture one or more mentoring relationships with trusted and knowledgeable colleagues and ask them to coach you on your interpersonal skills; reread Chapter 1, Communication; and read one or two books on the subject of social and emotional intelligence (see Recommended Reading List)

- *Communication skills.* These are different from and in addition to your basic social/emotional intelligence skills. These are the nuts and bolts of administrative communication—a shared vision for your school, decision making, emails and newsletters, effective meetings, the evaluation and documentation process, conflict management, protocol for speaking to the board, interaction with community and parent groups, schedules, schoolwide procedures and routines (including discipline), and the budget process.

  To develop these skills, attend classes and workshops that focus on communication skills; read professional journals and books; work with a mentor(s); and most important, reflect on what went well and what could have been different in every situation you encounter.

- *Reflection.* You cannot survive on impulse and decisiveness alone. You must take time to breathe and reflect on events as they occur. You *must* be able to identify and own your missteps as well as your successes. You will have both to contemplate. Be fair with yourself. Ask others for their perceptions and then use what they say. Reflect, reflect, reflect! Write your thoughts or process them with a trusted colleague. That's how you avoid off-the-cuff responses that get you in trouble. Describe a situation with clarity; identify the players, the barriers, and the points of influence; think about all the ways a situation could go and how you can impact the outcome.

- *Kindness/respect.* When you respect others, you receive respect in return. One act of kindness at a time can build a bank account of good will and trust that you will be able to access for a long time, and it keeps the bullies at bay. Remember that respect is aligned with communication, support, safety, competence, continuous renewal, and trust. You show true respect when you provide relevant support to your colleagues based on your competence in an area. You earn respect by becoming competent. Read books on kindness and respect for others (see Recommended Reading List).

- *Knowledge of learning theory and teaching methodology.* You are the instructional leader. You may not know all of the academic information contained in each course or at each grade level, but you must understand how students learn and be comfortable with identifying and using effective methodology. This you can learn from seeking advanced degrees, reading professional literature, attending professional conferences and workshops with or without your teachers, dialoguing with colleagues, and observing knowledgeable teachers. Sometimes administrators are relieved to know that they will no longer have to teach. We recommend that you never stop teaching. Offer to teach occasional lessons to hone your skills and to provide a model for others.
- *Organization/prioritization.* This one allows you and your staff to stay sane. When you are organized and able to prioritize, you create a climate where relaxed alertness prevails and productivity and creativity can become the focus. Consider the difference between orchestration and manipulation. The orchestra leader brings together musicians playing various instruments to perform a harmonious piece of music. In order to do this, he must provide the sheet music, chairs and music stands, schedules and places for practice and performances, his expertise in joining the sounds together, etc. He need not be expert in playing all instruments or knowledgeable about how to create and pay purchase orders, print the schedules, or rent the buildings. He merely needs to assure that all of these things are handled by knowledgeable people. He must pull everything together so that the sound is pleasing to the audience, the performers, and himself. Orchestration means creating cohesion, beauty, and harmony from initially unconnected elements.

  On the other hand manipulation seeks its own reward. A manipulative leader is likely to shuffle people, materials, and events to support her own power, to make herself look good. Find the "orchestra leaders" in your district and avoid the manipulators, observe them, offer to help them, and pick their brains. These are the people who can help you to become the kind of organizer and prioritizer that focuses on a harmonious outcome for everyone.
- *Systemic thinking.* Your school works systemically, i.e., what happens in classroom A impacts what happens in classroom B, the office, the

playground, the cafeteria, and the home. Nothing works in isolation. A teacher in charge of his own classroom, has some degree of control over the influence one event has on other events in the class. When you are the leader, you must be on the alert for events that impact other events on your campus. They are not as easy to spot as in the controlled environment of the classroom. You must be diligent. Any decision you make has ripples that extend much farther than you can imagine, so imagine as far as you can.

- *Shared vision.* Work with others to develop a unifying shared vision for everyone to hold close. Make sure every decision you make leads you in the direction of achieving the vision. Carry a picture of an excellent teacher and a happy, successful student in your head at all times, and that will help you to keep your focus on the vision.
- *Humility.* Jim Collins (2001) asserted in his book *Good to Great*: Great leaders give the credit to others. Their humility is so genuine and consistent that their names are often not even known outside their organizations. Those who work with these leaders recognize and appreciate their competence, but the leaders themselves do not seek recognition beyond the raised level of their self-efficacy. Satisfaction for these leaders comes in knowing that they have accomplished the task(s) they set out to accomplish rather than in receiving public acclaim. When this situation exists, the relationship circle is complete, and everyone within it succeeds.

Conversations with the Reader

A Walk on the Bright Side

Now it's your turn. Read the following story, and reflect on the ways **Leadership Connector, Competence** is demonstrated. See the questions at the end of this story to guide your reflection.

Brent

Brent began his career teaching high school math in the district he attended as a student from kindergarten through high school graduation. His goal was to become a school superintendent as quickly as he could. He taught for only three years before he was hired as his high school assistant principal in charge of facilities and operations. He became an assistant principal at the age of 27 in a school where he had been an honor student, student body president and an award-winning basketball player, and where his uncle still served as the venerated athletic director and football coach.

To some experienced administrators, Brent appeared to have almost insurmountable obstacles in his way. He was not only trying to establish himself as a competent administrator on a staff that included a highly regarded veteran who had known him since infancy, but he also had to pass muster with teachers who knew him first as a student. In a worst-case scenario he could be assigned to evaluate his uncle or discipline his former ASB advisor! Had he moved too fast without building the foundation of knowledge and experience he would need to meet this task? It seemed so.

But Brent liked a challenge. He wasn't daunted. He knew there was much he did not yet know. He had his master's degree, but he had to work on maintaining and increasing the respect of his colleagues. His wise principal assigned him to evaluate new teachers rather than veterans and to oversee custodians, groundskeepers, and campus security monitors. He handled a large number of student discipline cases as well. His assignment gave him the opportunity to show his competence to his colleagues, including his former teachers.

Brent kept his head down and went to work as he always had. Criticisms and complaints seemed to make him more committed to doing a good job. He listened, watched, reflected, and analyzed. He asked for clarification when he didn't understand the issue.

To culminate his year, he was in charge of the graduation ceremony, a highly visible assignment that could gain or lose him respect. He analyzed previous plans, recognizing that the ceremony and the venue had worked well in the past. Parking had always been a problem, so he made arrangements with nearby merchants to allow the use of their parking lots, and brought in shuttles to ease the movement from parked cars to the stadium. He made sure there was adequate supervision to allow students to celebrate but not to ruin the importance of their achievement. He ran efficient practices to help students feel confident about what they were doing. His popularity and reputation for fairness with students made the preparation congenial and painless. The event was a marvelous success.

After two years of proving himself, Brent's responsibility increased to include student assessment. All the while Brent volunteered for any assignments that would increase his competence in a variety of areas. When district administrative workshops were planned, he volunteered to attend. He finished the assigned reading first and eagerly contributed to all discussions. Finally, he enrolled in a well-respected doctoral program to prepare him for higher level administration.

He became principal of a middle school within two years and moved to another district after five years to become principal of an established high school. He is on his way to becoming a superintendent in the near future.

Reflective Questions

1. How would you describe Brent's approach to building his level of competence?
2. What worked?
3. What did he do that could transfer to your situation?
4. What surprised you in this scenario? What puzzled you?
5. What made you say "Aha!"
6. What would you do differently from Brent? Why?
7. Do you think Brent's staff is pleased to work at his school? Why?

Our Analysis

We would have predicted stumbles along the way for Brent as he began his administrative career without banking several years of experience in the classroom. Classroom experience is critical to teachers when they are deciding whether or not a new administrator is worthy of their respect and loyalty. In Brent's case, a unique pathway unfolded. We believe that his self-efficacy level was so high, it allowed him to take on the challenges and to enjoy success that no one could have predicted. It is clear that this pattern of believing in himself was nurtured from his youth and blossomed in adulthood.

Brent was raised with supportive mentors who guided him into successful decisions about his career. His social/emotional skills developed early and served him well in gaining the support he needed and in providing the same support to others. When he first became an administrator, he found a wonderful mentor in his principal who guided his career with pride and skill, showcasing Brent's organizational strengths for others and adding responsibilities as he proved himself. Brent did the organizational jobs at first—making sure facilities ran smoothly and important events succeeded. He never complained, only asked for more responsibility and more learning opportunities.

Brent took classes and enrolled in high-level programs at prestigious institutions, but most of his learning took place in his day-to-day work, building the relationships that could be mutually supportive. He got to know the superintendent, the assistant superintendents, and all of the maintenance workers. Everyone contributed to his learning. He saw worth in every person and honored everyone's knowledge, which soon became *his* knowledge. His communication with everyone was clear, respectful, and kind. People knew that they could trust Brent.

Every time Brent assisted a teacher with a discipline issue, made a visit to a student's home, assured the campus was clean, stopped a fight from occurring, or observed a skilled teacher teach a difficult concept, he strengthened his relationships with staff, students, and parents. Brent knew that when you pull one corner of the blanket, the rest of the blanket wrinkles and changes position. No action taken within an organization stands alone. Schools are systemic organizations, and Brent used that knowledge to increase success for everyone.

Most notably, humility for his accomplishments was instinctive with Brent. He made those around him want to work with him because he did everything he asked them to do and more. He owned his mistakes and learned from them. He was an example of someone who believed he could achieve a worthy goal and was willing to expend the effort it would take to accomplish the work.

A Walk on the Dark Side

Now read the next story and reflect on what went awry. See the questions at the end of this story to guide your reflection.

Greta

Greta had been a successful teacher for 15 years. She loved her students and her students loved her, but she was beginning to tire of all of the preparation she had to do as a teacher, and she wanted freedom from the daily schedule that imprisoned her in the classroom from one bell to the next. She longed for some time to plan her own day and to increase her salary for retirement. She went back to school and earned her administrative credential, accepting a job as an elementary principal in her own small district.

Greta dressed in a beautiful new suit and brought homemade cookies to the first staff meeting. She gained the immediate warm fuzzy reaction from her staff that she had hoped for. She continued to do thoughtful things for everyone whenever she saw the opportunity. She subbed for the first grade teacher when he wanted to watch his daughter receive an award at the middle school, she filled a basket with desk supplies for a new teacher, she visited classrooms often and listened to children read their stories to her, and she gave a fabulous Christmas party at her home for the entire staff. Everything seemed to be going well. Greta was happy.

And then teachers began to notice that some things were amiss.

- The fourth grade teachers ran out of supplies, and when they asked Greta to check on it, she assured them that she would, but no supplies arrived. When they repeated their request, Greta apologized, made them all cookies, and failed to provide the supplies once again.
- A parent called a fifth grade teacher at home and threatened legal action against him because he kept the child in the classroom during lunch. The teacher reported the incident to Greta who sympathized but decided to wait and see if the parent calmed down. He called the teacher again, even angrier, and Greta reassured the teacher that the parent would surely get over his concern. Eventually, the frustrated parent called the superintendent.
- The district hired an elementary physical education specialist to share between two schools. The schedule Greta submitted listed two classes during the same hour and placed first graders in P.E. during their lunch time. Greta apologized and submitted a new schedule that omitted one class and listed one class twice on a day that the specialist would be at the other school. She apologized again and turned the scheduling over to her administrative assistant.

At the end of the year when teachers celebrated an increase in test scores, Greta baked apple pies to celebrate. A hushed comment from one teacher to a colleague expressed the sentiment on campus—"Is baking her only strength? I'd rather have paper and pencils." Apple pies only confirmed staff perceptions that the test scores rose in spite of, not because of, Greta's expertise. Halfway through the next school year, the new superintendent moved Greta to the district office to develop curriculum and promoted the assistant principal to her position.

Reflective Questions

1. How is it possible for such a successful teacher to be incompetent as an administrator?
2. What conclusions regarding competence can you draw from this incident?
3. What could Greta have done differently?
4. What lessons, if any, could Greta have taken away from her experience as a principal?
5. How might Greta have rescued the situation?

Our Analysis

Greta had good intentions and excellent baking skills, but additionally her teachers needed her knowledge and support in areas of substance and relevance. Incompetence can easily be recognized when it is blatant and offensive. Greta loved her staff and the children. She simply did not search out resources that would help her gain the knowledge and learn the skills she needed or delegate the tasks that were difficult for her. Instead, she bumbled through with the assumption that apologizing would solve everything.

Let's look at Greta's competence in the areas we identified for administrative success:

- *Social/Emotional, Communication.* Greta knows how to interact with others pleasantly. She is probably great at a cocktail party making small talk, and she makes an initially good impression in her work, but she hasn't developed the skills that allow her to make people feel secure and confident that she can support them in areas relevant to their work.
- *Reflection, Systemic Thinking.* Greta does not appear to reflect on her actions. She often solves her problems with apologies, food, and gifts, a great beginning that needs to be followed by systematically clarifying situations, identifying possible outcomes, anticipating the effects on others, and taking remedial actions. If she followed these steps, she would reduce the need to apologize.
- *Learning Theory/Methodology.* We do not know much about her knowledge base as an instructional leader. Her students loved her, but that could just be because of her great chocolate chip cookies. This is an area in which an administrator cannot hand off expertise. While it is not necessary to know everything, it is critical to remain current through professional reading and dialogue, taking courses, and observing in classrooms to see what works, so she can support teachers in their work and encourage changes as necessary.
- *Organization/Prioritization, Shared Vision.* Greta's attempts to schedule P.E. classes suggest that she has difficulty with organization and prioritization. This is not a fatal flaw unless she fails to find someone to help her learn the skills. A principal whose aptitudes do not include clear organization needs an assistant principal and/or an administrative assistant who can assist in that area. There is no way to delegate building a shared vision to a colleague. The shared vision is based on knowledge of learning theory and instructional methodology. Vision and knowledge cannot be separated or delegated. Greta does not appear to have a shared vision in process. Without one, people flounder with no sense of purpose and direction.

- *Humility*. We think that Greta is humble, but she is humbled by her incompetence rather than by her accomplishments. The first is a debilitating type of humility that leads to reduced self-efficacy; the second is a satisfying sense of competence and increased self-efficacy.

We predict that, unless Greta learns to reflect and to develop her skills, administration will become burdensome and unsatisfying for Greta, and that she may return to the classroom where she found success, or she may even decide to leave the profession.

It's Your Turn

Now, we invite you to think about a situation in your experience in which **Leadership Connector, Competence** seemed to be strong or weak. You may wish to record your thoughts in a journal. Writing can help you think in more detail and focus, revealing truths you have not seen before. Or you may wish to reflect on the situation with a trusted friend to ask you clarifying questions and to summarize what he or she hears you say. The following questions and statements may help you to focus your thinking.

1. Describe the situation in as much detail as you can.
2. Who was involved and what roles did they play?
3. What fears did the participants seem to bring to the situation?
4. How was a positive outcome achieved or thwarted?
5. How could your level of competence have been increased?
6. What seemed to work well?
7. What could have been done differently to improve the outcome?

Critical Points to Remember about *Leadership Connector, Competence*

- There will always be more for you to learn, but there will always be a way for you to learn it.
- "I don't know" doesn't have to be an excuse. It can be a challenge to find out.
- Feeling good about yourself comes from believing you can do the task, preparing yourself to do it, and working hard to get it done, not from compliments from others.
- Administrative competence comes from developing skills in:
    - Social/emotional intelligence

- Communication
- Reflection
- Kindness and respect
- Knowledge of learning theory and methodology
- Organization and prioritization
- Systemic thinking
- Shared vision
- Humility.

Chapter 5

Leadership Connector, Continuous Renewal

> So long as a person is capable of self-renewal, they are a living being.
> *Henri Frederic Amiel*

Building Relationships with Your Mind, Body, and Soul

Just as leaders must take care of their teachers and staff, they must also take care of themselves. Too many young as well as veteran leaders are keeling over with heart attacks or have illnesses that debilitate them emotionally, psychologically, and/or physically. Many of the leaders that we have spoken to are on some type of medication including blood pressure, cholesterol, or anti-anxiety medication. The job of a leader should be one that brings joy, excitement, and validation to one's life. When outstanding leaders hear the clock ticking on 60 Minutes on Sunday evening, they, of course, wish the weekend had been longer; nevertheless, they relish the thought of another rewarding week at school. These leaders have a passion for and are committed to a healthy life, nurturing relationships with their families and friends, and their jobs.

Healthy leaders pay attention to the messages their bodies are sending them. They psychologically and physically support themselves; they ensure their mental and physical safety; they strive to keep themselves current and focus on continuous renewal. They cherish and protect the relationships they have with family and friends.

In this chapter, we highlight ways in which leaders can thrive, not just survive. We talk about the importance of **Leadership Connector, Continuous Renewal**. We focus on you, the leader. We focus on your well-being and ways in which you can continuously renew yourself. In this chapter we tend to use the pronoun "you" more than we have in other chapters because we encourage you to develop a relationship with yourself. We emphasize the critical need of (a) determining what battles are worth fighting, (b) being in close touch with your emotions, (c) engaging in reflection, (d) valuing and cherishing family, friends, and familiarity, (e) finding balance, (f) attending professional development, and (g) paying attention to your health. We begin this chapter with a scenario that demonstrates a leader's ability to determine when a situation just isn't worth fighting about.

Picking One's Battles

At 11:30 a.m. Mrs. Abernathy, a fifth grade teacher, came running into the office demanding to see the principal. She had just dropped off her students in the cafeteria. Although it was only the middle of the first month of school, Mrs. Abernathy had already determined that one of her students was a discipline problem. She didn't know what to do.

Mrs. Valero, the administrative assistant, immediately went to Principal Crockett's office to inform him of what was going on. Mrs. Abernathy followed right behind her. For the next minute Mrs. Abernathy ranted on and on. She demanded that something be done with this student by the end of the day. Mr. Crockett listened attentively and assured Mrs. Abernathy that he would help in any way possible. This assurance helped her to get control of her emotions. When she left his office, he reflected for a while and then wrote down some strategies that Mrs. Abernathy might use with this student.

He then proceeded to the cafeteria. He had realized a long time ago that lunch was an opportune time to talk informally with students and the cafeteria staff and to build relationships. He walked around and talked with the students and sat at various tables. Bobbie, Mrs. Abernathy's student, was at his table with his friends. Mr. Crockett talked to the boys about the Spurs Basketball Team, and when he left their table he reminded the boys to behave and have a great afternoon. He didn't speak specifically to Bobbie; he spoke to the entire group including the table next to Bobbie's. After lunch and throughout the afternoon, Mr. Crockett passed by Mrs. Abernathy's classroom to make sure everything was okay. It appeared that Mrs. Abernathy had calmed down after lunch, and, as a result, Bobbie had also calmed down.

At 2:45 after all of her students were on the bus, Mrs. Abernathy came to the office. She apologized for her actions that morning and asked Mr. Crockett if he had called the student to the office during lunchtime; she was really hoping that the principal hadn't done that. She was also concerned that he might have called the student's parents. She had taken care of the misbehavior and felt that she could handle her classroom discipline.

He hadn't confronted Bobbie nor had he called his parents. He knew that this was not a battle that needed to be fought with the teacher, the student, or the parent. He gave Mrs. Abernathy the latitude to solve the problem herself (knowing that she could) and had personally monitored the situation. He assured Mrs. Abernathy that everyone got frustrated at times and suggested that she reflect on the morning, determine what pushed her to the brink of her endurance, analyze how she felt reacting this way, and give some thought to what she would do if this reoccurred the following day. He then gave her the list of strategies he had written earlier in the day and said, "This morning after we spoke I wrote down some strategies you might use with Bobbie tomorrow. I don't know if you've tried any of these. When you get a minute look them over, consider which ones might work for you, and think about the ones that will not. I'll understand if you end up tossing them all. I want you to know that I support you, and I am here to help."

Mrs. Abernathy went home happy, as did Mr. Crockett. She returned early the next day and apologized once again. This opened the door for Mr. Crockett to reinforce what he had said the day before. He was able to stress proactive vs. reactive behaviors and the art of reflection.

Knowing When to Fight and When to Retreat

In the previous scenario, Mr. Crockett knew that the battle, which could have easily ensued, was not a battle that needed to be fought. Knowing which battles to fight and when you should back off can be difficult. You have to be in touch with your emotions, and you must have a strong knowledge and experiential base. Molehills can turn into mountains if you are not careful. Creating such mountains zaps your time and energy.

How do you know when to go to battle and when to retreat? How do you gain the knowledge you need in a short period of time, i.e., within one to three years? We have talked about being visible in **Leadership Connector, Support**. We can't emphasize enough how critical visibility is. To gain experience, one of our suggestions is to be vigilant about observing what is going on in your school. Observe, observe, observe. This strengthens your knowledge base and increases your experiential base. Successful leaders get to know their teachers. They are aware of the teachers who have great positive attitudes and handle their discipline well. They know their constant complainers. They observe what their teachers do and seek to find the reasons for their teachers' actions. One of our favorite quotes from Stephen Covey's *The 7 Habits of Highly Effective People* is, "Seek first to understand and then to be understood" (page 235). You can begin the process of understanding by observing, guiding, and supporting. Understanding what is actually going on enables you to determine the most meaningful way to respond to a person or a situation. Exemplary leaders use common sense, their knowledge, and their experience when situations present themselves.

As you observe, you are likely to come across situations that are certainly worth the battle. If a teacher is verbally or physically hurting a student, you have to act immediately; this is a battle worth fighting. We know of one principal who walked into a classroom and found a teacher holding a sixth grader against the wall by his shirt collar. It was evident that the student was struggling to get down. The principal quickly walked over to the teacher and said in a quiet yet firm voice, "Put him down now." She instructed the teacher to report to her office immediately. She called the assistant principal to the room to take over the classroom. She met with the teacher, took notes as the teacher spoke, and instructed the teacher to go home for the rest of the day. She then proceeded to call human resources for further guidance. The teacher was put on leave with pay, the parents filed a lawsuit, the paper got wind of the case, and the teacher left the district. This was worth going to the mat for.

You do not have to go to the mat if students are running off the bus, loitering in the halls, or screaming in the cafeteria. Nor do you have to engage in a battle if a teacher is constantly sending students to the office. Competent leaders work on these problems over time with the individuals involved. They don't have to magnify or intensify the situation. You can be present when the bus arrives and show students how to get off the bus. As you walk around the school, the number of loitering students is substantially diminished; it's funny how students find their classrooms when they see you in the halls! When a teacher keeps sending students to the office, you can work closely with that teacher by observing, being visible, and helping the teacher identify strategies to improve discipline.

We encourage you to think about other situations in which molehills easily become mountains. It's important to remember that students are required to be quiet, attentive, and engaged for long periods of time throughout the day, especially in the elementary grades. At the high school level a period may last for 50 minutes. During this time students are bound to the confines of their classrooms. Students have only a few minutes for interaction with their peers. By the time lunch rolls around, steam has built and students want and need interaction. As a result the cafeteria gets rather noisy, the halls get noisy, and the bus gets loud. This is normal; the effective leader rides with this tide and recognizes its flow. Of course, you don't want them screaming their lungs out; however, wise leaders welcome opportunities for students to dialogue and enjoy one another by simply talking. It is wise to avoid the "cafeteria is too loud, the halls are too loud, or the bus is too loud" battles. Let them talk. The entire day will be much better for all.

Exemplary leaders also determine which battles are worth fighting with parents. A good strategy is to treat them the way you want to be treated. Usually a screaming, irate parent just wants to be heard. There will be occasions when parents use curse words and say undesirable things about the teacher, the school, and you, the leader. This is when you must stop, listen, reflect, and then take positive action. Wise leaders do not tolerate this kind of behavior. Tell the parents that you really want to hear what the problem is and want more than anything to help the parent and the student; however, cursing and name calling aren't going to solve the problem. If the parent has made an appointment with you, invite the individuals involved to the meeting. The most effective way to work on the problem is to first talk with the teacher and anyone else involved at the school, get needed information, and then tell these individuals that you will provide them support during the meeting. If the individuals at the school have done something wrong, you need to work with them to determine how best to remedy the situation, how they will apologize to the student, how they will apologize to the parents, and how they will deal with situations proactively rather than reactively.

At times, you will be faced with horrendous challenges. We certainly don't want to minimize these; nevertheless, most problems are solvable if you have the pulse of your school, if you know your teachers' strengths and weaknesses, if your emotions are in check, and if you practice the art of reflection.

What Is Reflection and Why Is It So Important?

Have you ever sent an email and then realized that its impact would be negative? Have you ever said or done something impulsively that you wish you hadn't? We also have engaged in these types of reactive behaviors. When this has happened to us we have not been reflective. We attribute our blunders to being reactive versus proactive, not taking the time to think, taking things that people say and do too personally and letting our emotions spin out of control. Reflection certainly could have helped us in numerous situations.

In the last ten years much has been published about being a reflective practitioner. Like visibility, observing, and getting in touch with your emotions, we can't overstate the importance of reflecting before acting. Reflection is the art of purposefully thinking about what you have done and what you are going to do next. When we engage in reflection, it becomes much easier to make sense of our personal and professional worlds and how we operate in them; things become clearer. Reflective leaders conscientiously shy away from perseverating on problems and worrying about them. Perseveration and worry don't help a situation. If we thought they did, we would encourage you to try them. Instead, we encourage you to mull over and evaluate experiences in order to identify what worked. Then we encourage you to identify and examine what didn't work.

We have talked about observing what is happening at your site. Observing and then reflecting on what you have observed increases and enhances your knowledge base and your experiential base. A note of caution here regarding observing: It is very easy to slip from gathering information to judgment. Skilled leaders reserve their judgment until they have gathered data and then reflected on what those data mean. Before coming to a conclusion, we strongly suggest that you observe, reflect, and reflect again, and then come to a conclusion. So, as you walk through your building, talk with students and teachers, observe instruction, and work with parents and community, arrive at conclusions when you have data to support them. When we say data, we mean all sorts of data, discussions, observations, interactions, and written data.

You need to make a conscientious effort at purposeful reflection. Waking up at 2:00 a.m. with one's heart pounding or not being able to sleep doesn't help us, and, even more important, it's bad for a leader's health. For those who already engage in purposeful reflection—kudos! If you want to enhance your reflective skills we offer the following reflective strategies:

- *Be visible.* Talk with teachers, students, and staff each day. Take notes as you walk around your site. Identify ways in which you can improve the environment. Reflect on what you can do to make your school one in which everyone thrives, not just survives.
- *Keep a personal journal.* We know how busy and hectic your day can be, the time you take to reflect will surely benefit you. Reflection followed by being proactive will keep you out of trouble. You may want to avoid going from one situation to another and not learning from

the situation. The goals are to refrain from being judgmental, to learn from every situation, and to keep your emotions in tact.

- *Write Each Day.* Before you go home, sit down for ten minutes and write down the good, as well as the bad, that occurred during the day. Focus on the good first. This may be difficult. The productive thing about reflecting on the good first is that you don't beat up on yourself so much, and you find the good in people and events that we discussed earlier. Consider answering one or more of the following questions each day:
  - What made me pleased with my job today?
  - How did I help teachers, staff, students, and parents?
  - How did I enhance or build relationships today?
  - What went wrong today? What did I say or do that had a negative impact on someone or something?
  - Were my emotions in check?
  - Did I jump to conclusions?
  - If these events occurred again, what would I do differently?
  - What actions will I repeat again?
  - Which actions will I never repeat again?

Emotions

Emotions are funny things. They can help you to be kind, gentle, decisive, understanding, knowledgeable, and caring. Conversely, they can "eat you alive." When this happens, leaders tend to perceive life, people, and their jobs negatively. Emotions can breed contempt. They can cause you to be out of control and to do things that you will regret. Initially when you become a leader, your emotions seem to be unpredictable, but as you engage in the art of reflection and focus on your emotions, you will be able to predict your emotions and the emotions of others. As you think about emotions and the impact on your life, we offer you the following suggestions:

- *Identify what makes you happy.* What brings joy to your heart? Are you purposely looking for and engaging in actions that make you feel good about yourself and others around you? Perhaps you find pleasure in sitting in on an English class in which students are writing short stories and poems. You might even consider writing poetry on your own and think about how you might get it published. You might enjoy sitting with students and talking with them at lunchtime. This does wonders for discipline. You can go back to your office after lunch and relax since the office will not be full of students who have misbehaved at lunch. In addition, students, faculty, and staff appreciate you being there. These are the benefits you can reap from being visible.

We know of one principal who worked alongside her teachers and staff at a soup kitchen three days a week and felt completely validated about her purpose in life. The soup kitchen was right across the street from the school, and she, faculty and staff, were actively involved in assuring that her students got the best nutrition possible. The students ate breakfast and lunch at the school and were provided their dinner by the Benedictine Sisters at 4:00 each day. Many students would not have anything else to eat until the next morning at the school. Everyone at the school had developed a beautiful relationship with the kind Sisters. For the principal and many others, these relationships will last a lifetime. Helping others brought joy to their lives after a challenging day at school.

We know of another leader who sat with kindergarten students during art time and made the same art project they were making each week. The kindergarten students giggled when their work was better than the principal's! Parents called the school thanking the principal for spending time with their children.

If you don't know what makes you happy, do a little exploring. Some teachers may be reluctant to have you spend time in their classrooms, so the best thing to do is to hook on to the best teachers, let them know that you would like to come in and relax with the students, and then thank them via a note or card for their willingness to let you be a part of their classes. You might even consider thanking the entire class. You need not wear your heart on your sleeve; you just need to let them know you enjoy being with them. The key in all of these examples is to know what makes you happy and then go about doing whatever it is.

- *Determine what pushes your buttons.* Take time to sit down and ask yourself what aggravates you and examine why this happens. Ask yourself what you might conscientiously do to deal with these stressors. Keep a journal. Have you done everything you possibly can to get control of your emotions? Have you made attempts to develop relationships with people who get on your nerves? Once you know what pushes your buttons, you will be able to improve relationships with these people.
- *Engage in dialogue and reflection with a trusted friend.* This individual should not be a co-worker or associated with your work. Ask your

friend to tell you how he or she views the situation at hand. It's important to examine emotions rather than bottle them up inside.

- *Consider attending conferences.* Seek out conferences on emotional intelligence, conflict resolution, and stress management. These conferences help you to continuously renew yourself. It is important to know that others share the same frustrations, but it is also important to find ways in which you might deal with conflict and stress. All leaders want to be intelligent. What is most important is that leaders are emotionally intelligent.
- *Concentrate on your own professional development.* This is as important for you as it is for teachers and staff at your site. Teachers and staff will see you as a role model. Carefully cull through what is available. Select and participate in professional development activities that provide you with what you need. Look for meaningful learning opportunities that will enrich you. Present what you have learned at a faculty meeting. Let your teachers know how you will use this knowledge and how it will impact you and them. Discuss what you now know with your district supervisor. Consider presenting this information to your principal colleagues. Discuss how they might integrate this information into their practice.
- *Take a walk.* When the emotions start to bubble and they seem overwhelming, take a brisk walk around the school and breathe deeply. This may sound a little basic, but it works. As you walk, try not to let the emotions get the best of you. Think of what makes you happy. Think of a trip you have recently taken, think of your children, think of some amusing incident, or count backwards from 500. The goal is to get your mind off whatever is occurring so that (a) you calm down, (b) you reflect, and (c) you come up with a solution to the problem. You can revisit the situation once you have calmed down. You will then increase your chances of proceeding proactively.
- *Be conscious of your attitude.* Attitude is everything. Attitude has a wonderfully unique way of controlling a leader's emotions. Develop a mantra. When you greet individuals, come up with a response that seems to fit you best when individuals ask, "How are you?" You might respond with "I'm super," "I'm great," "Grand," "Couldn't be better," "Superb." Just pick or identify one response and say it all the time. Before you know it, you will feel great, grand or superb, and others will identify you with your positive descriptor. Positive thinking and proactive behaviors are powerful.

- *Find the good in everyone and everything.* Tell yourself constantly that you will. We know that this is tough; the alternative is not a good one. When you have found the good in someone, tell him. Tell the teacher how much you enjoy her smile when she walks into the building. Praise teachers for excellent classroom management, having grades in on time, their rational thinking, always being willing to help, having a clean classroom, and/or the ease with which they begin or dismiss their classes. Find a way to celebrate individuals by finding the good in them. Their reaction toward you will be positive; they will appreciate your action and may even remember it. This is a good coping mechanism for interacting with people about whom you may have negative feelings.

- *Be patient.* Good leaders are patient with people and recognize that they themselves must exhibit patience first if they want others to be patient with them. Patience requires a conscientious effort to examine situations and ask yourself what is going on. Resonating within us must be the words, "I need to be patient, I need to be patient. Everything works out so much better when I'm patient." Successful leaders know that impatience with people and situations is transparent. Teachers easily identify an impatient leader. Impatience stirs up negative emotions and breeds more impatience.

- *Focus on organization.* Being organized helps to keep our emotions in check. Frustration abounds when we're running late, when we can't find a document and have to search through stacks of paper, when we haven't answered emails for two days, when we haven't decided ahead of time what to buy at the grocery store, or what will be for dinner that night. We know of one principal who was so disorganized and stressed that he went to school wearing a brown shoe and a black shoe. Frustration results in stress and seems to snowball into negative emotions. Successful leaders are organized, their offices are organized, and their lives are organized.

  We know of one principal who gets his clothes ready for the week. He has his shirts, slacks, ties, jackets, shoes, belts, and underwear ready on Sunday for the entire week. He justifiably brags about how he gets up each morning, eats, showers, and dresses within 30 minutes. He confides that he doesn't have time for "clothing stressors" in the morning. On Friday morning he leaves his clothes in a bag at his front door and the dry cleaner picks them up and drops them off late Saturday afternoon. If you're thinking this may be a little too much organization, give it more thought. What can you do to organize your life and your work?

Understanding your emotions, identifying what makes you happy, determining what pushes your buttons, concentrating on your own professional development, and being organized will certainly help you to continuously renew yourself. You'll become a better leader!

Friends, Family, and Mobility

Friends and family tell a lot about us. In many ways they help to define who we are, what we are, and what we believe. Similar likes and dislikes, being with one another, and sharing special moments all help us to be healthier and happier. When our friends and extended family are physically close by, our lives are more complete. When you have companionship, a helping hand, and emotional support you are less likely to be isolated. Your life will be psychologically more fulfilled because you have anchors to keep you steady.

You should exercise caution when contemplating moving to another city, state or even another district. Taking the first job that comes along and not reflecting on its potential impact on you, family, and friends, may prove to be detrimental to you and everyone you care about. Guard yourself against falling into the "first job offer trap." What we mean here is that often that first job seems glamorous. We become overwhelmed with happiness when we land that first position as an assistant principal, a principal, an assistant superintendent, or superintendent. Give that potential first job careful and deliberate thought. Discuss the job with those close to you. That first job will make or break your reputation. Sure, you will get another job, but what you did in your first job always follows you, whether in your mind or in the minds of others.

Exemplary leaders do some investigating before accepting a job, especially if the job requires moving or suffering long commutes. Yes, suffering. Long commutes just aren't fun. They deplete our energy and the time we have to spend with those we love. Long hours behind the wheel of a car aren't healthy either. The following questions might help you decide if you should move to accept a leadership position, accept the first job you are offered, or suffer that long commute.

- Go online and find out everything you possibly can about the district and the school. Look at the department of education's website. What are the district's achievement test results? What are the school's test results?

- Either through questions or what you find online, determine how principals are supported in this district. Does the district supply resources that will enable you to purchase what the school and teachers need? What professional development is available to principals, teachers, and staff in this district?
- What forms of communication exist in the district and school? Were there problems with the school's previous leader? Are there newsletters, uniform parent communiqués, or other forms of communication?
- Read the area's local newspapers for at least two weeks. Are the schools mentioned? Are the district and schools viewed in a positive light?
- If you are going to move, go shopping at the local grocery store. How did you feel in the store? Did the store meet your expectations regarding cleanliness, products, and service? Do you think you could develop and enjoy a relationship with the individuals in the store? Identify the location of the dry cleaner, gas station, hospital, drugstore, and restaurants. Are they in reasonable distance of where you are thinking of moving? Ask a real estate agent about the district and schools. If you or your children have specific medical needs, can doctors and medical personnel in the immediate area meet them?
- Be sure to reflect on the interview. Does the chemistry seem right? Reflect on what resonated with you during the interview. Did you feel comfortable? Who put you at ease? How much power do they wield in the school and district? If there were individuals that made you feel uncomfortable, reflect on the reasons why. How much power do they wield? Can you be successful in this position if you have to interact with them?
- Are the people that you value and cherish (specifically family) eager for you to accept this job? What do they have to say? Will you be able to spend time with them? If not, will you someday regret not having done so?

Careful reflecting on and honestly answering these questions will pay off. Be wise and take a careful look before you leap. There might be a position in your district or in neighboring districts. Look at these positions first. Moving and commuting long distances can have some serious repercussions.

Finding Balance

Life cannot be all work or all play. There has to be a balance and at times a separation of the two. We know of many leaders who spend evenings and weekends doing work-related tasks. Their lives and their relationships with family and friends suffer. Clearly they need balance. Balance requires organization. It takes time and energy to figure out how one can organize and balance the 24-hour day.

Charlene, a high school principal, has organization down to a science. She suggested to us that her secret began years ago by identifying her optimal time during the day to get the most work done. Charlene is a morning person. She gets up early in the morning (approximately 4:30–5:00 a.m.) and begins her day by thinking about the things she has to do. She writes out a plan each morning, drinks her two cups of coffee, exercises (she's too tired to do that at night), showers, gets dressed, and reads an article to be sure she is current. She wakes her children at 6:30 and makes sure they are on the bus at 7:20. Her children know the morning schedule and abide by it because it makes the day better for everyone. She leaves at the same time they do. She basically begins the school day in the same way, planning the day, answering emails and phone calls, walking the halls, talking with teachers and students. Her assistant principals know exactly what she expects; this they very much appreciate. She and her assistants focus on a safe and clean environment, classroom management, and instruction. She worked very hard on a discipline code with the faculty and provides support when they need it. Students aren't outside her office or the assistant principals' waiting to be disciplined. There is a discipline code, and it is enforced.

Evidence of her organization and balance is in her spotless office. The mounds of papers one might find in the offices of other leaders simply do not exist in her office. Her administrative assistant separates her daily mail into three stacks: URT=Urgent Do Today, FTW=Finish This Week, and NBD=No Big Deal. She tackles the mail after her morning walk-through and after she has had time to talk with her assistant principals. Each morning she finds out what she can do to support them in their work. After her discussions with them, she takes care of the URT file and then walks through the school again. She visits the cafeteria and then works on more email, phone calls, FTW, or whatever project she is working on. The school is organized and balanced. At 5:00 p.m. she gets in her car to go home. At 5:30, like clockwork, she and her children make dinner. By 6:30, her children are doing homework; she is reading the paper, watching television or doing what needs to be done at home. By 9:30 she is reading a book in bed and by 10:00 she is fast asleep.

We were quite surprised by her daily routine and regimen. When we told her it sounded like boot camp, she replied, "Being a high school principal is really tough. You can't do it unless you are very well organized. At the high school level, you can't fly by the seat of your pants. Your assistants have to know clearly what you expect. If you want to raise achievement, you don't have time to spend on discipline. That's why we got together (even the crabby teachers and the ones who think they are the next best thing to sliced bread) and developed a discipline code. The agreement was that everyone would participate, abide by the code, and reap the benefits. I had to do many, many workshops for them on classroom management; I had to guide and facilitate the process; it took almost a year to make it work, but now we focus on teaching and learning. They can predict what I will do in a situation, and I can predict what they will do because we are on the same page. Don't get me wrong, I have some teachers that keep me hopping, and there are times when I have to put my foot down, but I have been successful in developing relationships with them so they know me, and I know them. They know what I mean when I say, 'We are in the business of teaching and learning.' They also know that I don't expect them to stay after school until 5:00 or 6:00 each night. I want them to have balance too. I want them to enjoy life, enjoy their families, work on being healthy, and give me their best when they are here at school. I do and I think they should too."

We asked Charlene how she managed home life. She said, "Do you mean things like cooking and cleaning? Well, I don't make millions, but I make a good salary. I pay a very honest and reliable person to come in and clean for me. I have my dry cleaning picked up and delivered, and I love to cook. If on weekends I'm feeling crazed from the week or if I had an outstanding week, I end up cooking up a storm and freezing food. We go out for pizza on Fridays. If need be, I bring home prepared food from the supermarket. This really helps me when I have to go back for an evening event. Our house is clean, and we enjoy life. We have made a pact to not worry about the small stuff. When I am overtaxed, I stop and reflect. I adjust my schedule in the morning and keep on going. Thinking about, but not worrying about things, helps me tremendously. I know all of this sounds easy, but you have to be organized in order to keep balance in your life. What's the alternative? I am in charge of a high school that has an enrollment of over 3,500 kids. If I weren't as organized as I am, if I didn't have a balanced life, the high school would be a wreck, I'd go bananas, and my family wouldn't be there to support me."

We had a great time interviewing Charlene. This is what we learned from her about balance in one's life:

- Identify the time of day when you are at your best. It might be 5:00 a.m. or 10:00 p.m. Plan your day if you are an early riser or plan the following day if you are a night owl. Planning puts you in control.
- Organize life, family, and job.
- Exercise each day.
- Read to keep current, and also read for relaxation and pleasure.
- Keep your office clean. Don't let stacks of paper pile up. This only causes stress, and you will probably end up taking work home.
- Enlist the help of your administrative assistant with the mail. Have her use a system for separating the mail. Charlene's system of URT, FTW, and NBD worked very well for her. Enlist your administrative assistant for all other help that you deem appropriate.
- Make sure the assistant principals, teachers, and staff know exactly what you expect. This way you don't have to fight battles because people don't know what they should or shouldn't be doing.
- Focus on improving discipline so you don't use your time taking care of discipline problems. Conduct workshops or find a competent presenter to do so.
- Focus on teaching and learning instead of constantly putting out fires.
- Spend money on cleaning services for your home. Time is a precious commodity.

Never Underestimate the Value of Your Health

A wise university professor would always have a lengthy discussion with his doctoral students who were all practicing school leaders. He would ask his doctoral students to take out a piece of scrap paper and prioritize the following three words: *family*, *health*, and *job*. Students were asked to write down the reasons for their prioritizations. He instructed the students to take five minutes for this exercise during which time they were not permitted to talk; they were required to think and reflect. After the five-minute period elapsed, he asked each student to tell the group which came first, second, third, and why. He tallied their responses on the board. For many the first priority was family. For many others the first was job. Only a very few listed health as their Number 1 Priority.

This professor was never surprised by the results. He was always dismayed that things had not changed much over the years. His suggestion was to rethink priorities. He strongly believed, as we do, that health should come first, followed by family, and then job. His rationale for this prioritization was as follows: First, if an individual is not healthy he cannot take care of himself, his family, and his job. Second, if an individual does not have a good relationship with family, his health and job will suffer. Third, a job is a job; your success at that job depends on being emotionally, psychologically and physically healthy, and happily involved in relationships with family and friends.

We encourage you and your family to engage in this reflective exercise. We encourage you to talk about your assumptions, regarding life, health, family, friends, and job.

We have learned to put health above all else. Many leaders, more than we like to admit, tell us that they don't have time to think about their health, it never crosses their minds, they expect to be tired and run down since they have tough jobs, they are okay; it is just the stress of the job, the job is too important, they don't want to lose their jobs, and the list goes on and on. We often ask them how important the job will be if they are incapacitated or worst yet, DEAD. We don't intend, nor would we ever minimize, the importance of jobs to leaders; however, we only pass this way once. Putting health on hold will come back to haunt you at some point. This is a good juncture to take a walk on the bright side.

Conversations with the Reader

A Walk on the Bright Side

Now it's your turn. Read the following story, and reflect on the ways **Leadership Connector, Continuous Renewal** is demonstrated. See the questions at the end of the story to guide your reflection.

Samantha

It was a beautiful Monday morning at Weber Middle School. Ms. Samantha Logan, the principal was answering email and checking her schedule for the day when she heard the front door slam. Someone was screaming. She jumped out of her chair and ran to the front office. At the counter was Mrs. Fielden, parent of a seventh grader, screaming at the administrative assistant. Ms. Logan immediately asked Mrs. Fielden how she could help. She responded, "Someone has stolen my kid's gym clothes, and you better do something about it. I am sick and tired of what goes on at this school. Kids do whatever they want, and nobody cares." Ms. Logan turned to Mrs. Fielden and said, "What size are his gym clothes?" Mrs. Fielden grumbled,

"Richie is a size 14." Ms. Logan responded, "I think I can help. Would you excuse me for just one minute?" She offered Mrs. Fielden a cup of coffee.

Ms. Logan returned with brand new size 14 gym clothes. She had developed a network with a number of middle school principals. They took care of one another and anticipated what they would need throughout the school year to head off problems. They saw to it that each had a few extra gym clothes in various sizes. When she handed Mrs. Fielden the clothes, she said, "Here are some new gym clothes. We'll find out what happened to Richie's clothes. Have a great day, and I'll get in touch with you as soon as I have an answer." Mrs. Fielden's attitude changed immediately. She thanked Ms. Logan for her help and left.

At lunchtime Ms. Logan made a point to see Richie in the cafeteria. She had a great rapport with the students and frequently sat at their tables to eat and talk with them. She was one of the few principals in the entire district who knew all 900 students by name and, equally important, she was one of the very few who was familiar with their home lives. When she sat at Richie's table, she was able to comfortably ask him about the gym clothes. Richie had no idea what happened to his clothes since last week. He thought they were at home, but he couldn't find them. He kept asking his Mom where they were, and according to Richie, "She got mad and started screaming at me." He said, "Mom, maybe somebody stole them," and according to Richie, once again, "She went ballistic." Richie was so glad that she wasn't mad at him anymore; she focused her anger on the imaginary student who had stolen his clothes.

Ms. Logan asked Richie if his clothes might be in his locker. He didn't know. Together they went to his locker. It was a big mess! Ms. Logan couldn't believe her eyes. She asked Richie to empty his locker. When it was almost a third empty, Richie exclaimed, "Hey, there's my gym stuff!" They put all of his things back in his locker. Richie promised to take better care of his gym clothes and offered to take home some of the junk that was in his locker.

When Ms. Logan returned to the office, there was a message to call the superintendent. Immediately numbness took over her body. Could Mrs. Fielden have gone to his office to complain about her? She had butterflies in her stomach as she dialed his extension. When the superintendent got on the phone, he said, "Samantha, you are doing a great job at Weber Middle. A parent came to my office raving about you and how you helped her. She said she was going through a divorce right now, and things were really tough. Thanks, Samantha for all you do at Weber and for our district."

Samantha was so relieved and ecstatic that things had gone so well. She was happy that she was reflective instead of reactive. When Richie went home, he told his Mom about Ms. Logan having lunch with him and his friends. He was elated that she helped him. Ms. Logan had a wonderful relationship with Mrs. Fielden for the rest of Richie's career at Weber.

Reflective Questions

1. How would you describe Ms. Logan's emotional state of being?
2. What did she do when she heard someone screaming?
3. Describe the relationship she had with Richie and with Richie's Mom?
4. How were these particular relationships developed?
5. What worked in this situation? What did she do that you could transfer to your situation?
6. What did Ms. Logan do that surprised you in this scenario? What puzzled you?

Our Analysis

Ms. Logan began her day by making good use of time. She was in the process of answering her email and checking her schedule. She immediately responded to the screaming she heard in the front office. She did so proactively. Instead of saying, "Why are you screaming?" she asked how she might help the parent. Ms. Logan was in control of her emotions and did a superb job of displaying her own emotional intelligence. Mrs. Fielden, the parent, was loud, abusive, and accusatory; nevertheless, Ms. Logan persevered. She did not take things personally, which is hard to do. She acted as a reflective practitioner. She reflected quickly on what she might do to solve the problem and proceeded to follow through. She even went as far as offering Mrs. Fielden a cup of coffee.

Ms. Logan had developed relationships with other middle school principals. They supported one another, reflected on problems they might encounter during the year, and planned a course of action. As a result, she was able to solve this anticipated problem within a few minutes.

Ms. Logan recognized the importance of being visible. She had developed a rapport with the students and was welcomed in the lunchroom. She was able to talk to Richie and go to his locker with him without students taunting him. Richie even promised to take home some of the things in his messy locker.

You never know what parents will do. In this particular case, the parent's adrenaline was really flowing. Anything was possible. Because Ms. Logan kept her emotions in check, the parent wasn't provided any sparks to fuel a potential fire. Ms. Logan knew that this was not a battle worth fighting. Mrs.

Fielden went to the superintendent's office to praise Ms. Logan. Richie went home and praised Ms. Logan. Ms. Logan built relationships rather than engage in battle.

A Walk on the Dark Side

Now read the next story and reflect on what went awry. See the questions at the end of this story to guide your reflection.

Max

Max had been a great biology teacher for 20 years. He was well liked by the teachers, his principal, and vice principal. When the superintendent came to visit his high school, she always made sure she stopped by his classroom to tell him and his students what a great teacher he was.

Max had been working on his administrative credential at a nearby university and was encouraged to pursue an assistant principalship. He found his first position in a high school located two hours away from his home. This would mean a four-hour roundtrip commute. He would have to leave early in the morning to avoid traffic and would have to wait till the traffic dissipated before he started the trek home. He and his wife talked about moving to the district. After many, many deliberations, Max decided that he was going to commute. His wife had a job she loved, and his kids had a few more years until they finished high school. He decided that he would leave at 5:30 each morning and drive back home each day at 6:00 p.m.

For three years, things worked out beautifully. He started his new job at the age of 42, was healthy, and enjoyed the commute. Each day, he welcomed the opportunity to reflect on his way to and from school. He bought a tape recorder and talked aloud to himself, reflecting first on all that went well that day and all that he could have done differently. He planned his day and week as he drove back and forth. During his third year he wrote a grant that really put his school on the map. In the evenings when he got home, he would work on school matters. He loved his job! He was on curriculum committees, was involved in starting the district's school business partnership, was visible throughout the day, and was available when teachers, staff, and parents needed him. He closely resembled Superman; he was everything to everyone.

He continued at this pace for another two years. In his mind, he was a proud example of what one could become if an individual worked hard and concentrated on developing relationships even if one had to spend long hours commuting. People forgot, or just didn't think about his living so far away. He was always available for football games and other athletic events.

The debate team loved him. Going to away events was no problem for him. He gave them his heart, body, and soul.

During his five-year tenure at the high school, there were three different principals. When the third principal left, Max toyed with the idea of applying for the principalship; however, he was very content in his position and decided against it.

At the end of the fifth year everything changed. The district decided to appoint Milt as the interim principal instead of hiring a new principal. Milt was also a principal at a neighboring high school. The superintendent expected Milt to divide his time between the two high schools; Milt's salary would also increase because of his extra high school duties. Milt came into the high school ready to change everything. He was known for tightening the purse strings and to the dismay of everyone, including Max, Milt was notorious for micromanaging. He didn't care who he ran over. He told everyone in the school what he wanted and when he wanted it. If someone dared to trespass against his wishes he would tell the person that minute or send Max as the messenger to deliver the reprimand or bad news. Max was often the go-between. Milt was extremely shrewd and downright mean.

Max worked hard to strengthen the relationships he had developed over the years, and at the same time Max made every attempt to garner the support of this interim principal. There were days that Milt chewed Max out to the point that he could not eat or sleep. He couldn't believe this was happening to him. He was kind, gentle, rational, logical, and hard working. People liked him. What could he do about Milt? This interim principal had turned the school upside down. He couldn't go to the new assistant superintendent; he didn't want to sound incompetent or whiny. Teachers avoided Milt as much as possible. The teachers were afraid of Milt so they hesitated to speak negatively about him except in the teachers' lounge or at parties. Milt was the "superintendent's boy." He liked Milt; he wouldn't do anything.

Max was shocked that the climate and even the school's organizational culture had changed dramatically in just one year. Max made it through that year, but he started to feel run down. He was always tired, and it seemed that everything hurt. In June, Max was feeling chest pains. He knew he hadn't been eating right and slacked off on his exercise regimen. He kept asking himself what he could do to make things better.

During the first week of July, he had a heart attack. He was confined to rest for most of July, and in August he began cardiac rehabilitation. In September, he went back to work and worked as hard as he had the previous six years. He was only 48; he felt he could do it. Meanwhile, Milt was renewed for another interim year, and his salary increased substantially once again.

This year he started to give Max 99% of his duties. Max's life became much harder. He found himself consumed with schoolwork on the weekends. He was now doing two jobs, his and the principal's. He missed his wife and family who seemed so far away, yet he saw them every evening. He longed to be with them, but work had taken over and was his first priority. His wife and children pleaded with him to find a job (any job) closer to home. There were a number of positions within minimal commuting distance for which Max could apply. Max decided to stick it out against the wishes of his family.

In mid-October Max felt chest pains once again. At first, he ignored them thinking that it was indigestion. He wasn't watching his diet as he had in July and August; he slacked off on exercising again. On, Friday he went home early because he wasn't feeling well. He had a stroke on Sunday. At the age of 48 his administrative career ended.

Reflective Questions

1. How would you describe Max's approach to his commuting distance?
2. How would you describe Max's approach to his job? How did Max prioritize his life?
3. How did Max develop relationships?
4. What worked in this situation?
5. What went wrong? What would you do differently?
6. What surprised you in this story? What puzzled you?
7. If you had a chance to speak to Max, what would you say?

Our Analysis

Max began his journey as a school leader at the age of 42. The superintendent recognized his talents as a teacher. She went out of her way to acknowledge him when she was in his building. His relationships at the school were solid and sustained. He had developed a fine reputation and was very marketable. In order to fulfill his desire to become a school leader he completed the requirements for an administrative credential. He followed the advice of his professors and applied for leadership positions. It would have been wise for Max to meet with the superintendent or let her know during one of her visits that he was taking courses at the university and would be applying for positions in the future.

Max took his first job as an assistant principal in a district that was far away from his home. Max would have ultimately fared much better if his position had been closer to home and his family. Arriving home at 7:00 or 8:00 in the evening robs a leader of precious time with his family, friends, and himself. Max can never reclaim or relive all the time that he lost. He fell into the "first job trap!"

Max was a young, energetic, and charismatic man whose body was able to tolerate the commute for five years. As a matter of fact, he loved his job until the interim principal arrived. Things changed drastically, and that is when he should have reflected and asked himself what he could do for himself. He tried to work with Milt, the interim, but that was not ever going to pan out. Milt wasn't going to change. Milt wasn't going to leave. Milt lived in the district and was buddies with the people in the community. Max would have been wise to look for another job closer to home. If there are any signs of a potential problem, it is always best to leave when you are flying high. Once a leader gets caught in someone else's mess, the leader becomes part of the mess, and that's simply not good.

Max missed the telltale signs that his life was not balanced. He put his work above all else. He was overworking his mind and body. He lost his relationship with himself. When the pains started, they should have been a wake-up call. When Max had the heart attack, he completely and utterly missed that call also. He made it worse by going back to his high school in September. It would have been better to go back to teaching in his home district. Yes, it is said that you can never go back; but you can, and it is perfectly alright to do so!

It's Your Turn

Now, we invite you to think about a situation in your experience in which **Leadership Connector, Continuous Renewal** seemed to be strong or weak. You may wish to record your thoughts in a journal. Writing can help you think in more detail and focus, revealing truths you have not seen before. Or you may wish to reflect on the situation with a trusted friend to ask you clarifying questions and to summarize what he or she hears you say. The following questions and statements may help you to focus your thinking.

1. Describe the situation you have selected in as much detail as you can.
2. Who was involved and what roles did they play? What role did you play?
3. What beliefs did the participants bring to the situation?
4. How well did you know the participants involved?
5. Describe your emotions in this situation.
6. Describe the emotions of the participants.
7. How did you arrive at your conclusions?

8. What seemed to work well?
9. What did not work well?
10. Describe the relationship you have with your body, mind, and soul.
11. What could have been done to improve the outcome? In what ways were relationships built or destroyed?
12. How can the broken relationships be rescued? If they can't, why not?

Critical Points to Remember about *Leadership Connector, Continuous Renewal*

- Develop a relationship with yourself. Know thyself.
- Pick and choose your battles carefully. Making mountains out of molehills zaps your energy and plays games with your mind.
- Make a conscientious effort to know the people, students in your building, parents, and the community. Knowing these individuals helps you know when to go to battle and when to retreat.
- Know what makes you happy and what pushes your buttons. Reflect on how you can get your emotions in check.
- Emotions can help you to be kind, gentle, decisive, understanding, knowledgeable, and caring. On the other hand, they have the potential to wreak serious havoc with your mind and body. Negative emotions can breed contempt and "eat you alive."
- Attitude is everything.
- Don't take all things personally. We know this is difficult, but try your best.
- The art of reflection helps you make sense of all that goes on in your school.
- Observe, reflect; observe, reflect; observe, reflect. Examine all data and then arrive at conclusions.
- Do not accept the first job that comes along unless you have seriously examined how the position will affect you and your family. Long commutes can be detrimental to you and your health.
- Be cognizant of how you balance your life. Ask yourself how you personally prioritize health, family, and job. Ask yourself why.
- Your health should always be your first priority. Pay attention to aches and pains. They could be serious. See your doctor and make the needed changes in your life.

Chapter 6

Leadership Connector, Trust

> Trust men and they will be true to you; treat them greatly and they will show themselves great.
> *Ralph Waldo Emerson*

Trust Is Precious

Leadership Connector, Trust is the most important part of any relationship, and at the same time, it is the most vulnerable and sensitive. Trust takes substantial time, energy, and commitment to the person or group whose trust a leader seeks. Trust is precious. It takes weeks, months, even years to develop and sustain. One of the most astonishing parts about trust is that it can be destroyed in seconds, in just a word, in just a sentence, or in one action. In order to be trusted, leaders must constantly evaluate what they are about to say and do and what they have done. Leaders need to do this because of the fragile nature of trust.

We have been asked why we put trust near the end of the book rather than at the beginning. We have purposely placed trust in this chapter because in order to be trusted and to trust others, the **Leadership Connectors, Communication, Support, Safety, Competence, and Continuous Renewal** must be present at all times. These Leadership Connectors must be the foci of everything the leader does.

Teachers and students will question your trust if your **Communication** does not connect them to you. If a leader does not openly and honestly communicate with individuals, trust wanes. If a leader is threatening, harsh, or deceptive, trust dies. **Support** is a vital part of trust. If the leader does not identify, validate, and meet the needs of teachers, trust collapses. Teachers expect, and rightfully so, their leader's financial and human support. **Safety** is as important as each of the other Connectors. A leader will not be trusted if she does not focus on the emotional, psychological, and physical safety of teachers, staff, and students. These individuals need to know that they can go about their jobs of teaching and learning in a caring and safe environment. They need to know that their leader has their best interests at heart. **Competence** strengthens relationships and fosters trust when teachers and staff believe that the leader knows what she is doing. Teachers will hesitate to trust the leader if she lacks the knowledge, skills, and dispositions to assist teachers, staff, and students. Leaders must demonstrate their emotional intelligence. **Continuous Renewal** also determines whether or not a leader will be trusted. If the leader (a) has her emotions in check, (b) is proactive versus reactive, (c) is reflective, (d) engages in professional development, (e) engages in activities that promote her own emotional, psychological, and physical well-being, (f) cherishes and nurtures family and friends, and (g) finally recognizes that health comes first and that no job is worth dying for, then the chances of trusting and being trusted are much more probable.

In order for **Leadership Connector, Trust** to be present, all of the other Connectors must be present. One Connector is as important as another; they are all interrelated and interdependent. If a leader neglects or damages one of the Connectors, there is a disconnect and trust falters.

In this chapter we focus on Trust and its importance in developing meaningful, purposeful, and long-lasting relationships. We explore the concept of trust by examining (a) respecting versus liking, (b) honesty, (c) caring and taking care of others, (d) valuing strengths, (e) respecting privacy, and (f) betrayal and the feelings that surface when betrayed. All of the Connectors are embedded in these topics.

Respecting Versus Liking

We have talked about the importance of treating everyone with dignity and respect. We all come from different backgrounds with different ways of looking at people, of perceiving what is happening, and of evaluating how one fits into the overall scheme of things. Throughout life and our leadership careers, we will always encounter people who look different from us, have different ideas, have different dispositions, have more or less knowledge and skills than we, and perceive and judge differently. Recognizing these concepts makes life easier for the leader. We don't have to like everyone or agree with everyone, but as leaders, first and foremost, we have to respect everyone. A wise leader broadens her own narrow space in life, letting others in, while searching for the universal dimensions of her school. Letting in people who are different and embracing who they are sets the stage for becoming a true team.

Leadership is about teamwork. It is about respecting an individual's human right to be different. Leadership is about bringing everyone together in a focused, safe, supportive, and communicative learning community. There must be a transparent environment in which people feel part of a team that recognizes their values and contributions. Trust flourishes in this type of environment.

A Cautionary Note

We know of one principal who *talked* about everyone being part of the school and working together. She, along with the teachers, decided to apply for the Distinguished School Award in her state. Initially things progressed smoothly. At the first meeting, everyone was on board ready to go forward with their leader. A good discussion ensued, and excitement filled the room.

At the second planning meeting, Stephanie brought doughnuts, Jennifer brought soda, and Angela Kay brought the big Post-it butcher-block paper and markers. The principal remarked, "These doughnuts are good, but I wish you had brought something healthy." Everyone just looked at her. Amy thought that wasn't very nice, but didn't hold the thought for long. Next the group talked about which parents, teachers, and community members they would include in the process. The principal voiced her disapproval of every individual that teachers suggested. The committee members, once again, looked at the principal. They were surprised at her frankness and disrespect for so many individuals who were directly related to the school.

Things seemed to get worse by the minute. To change the topics of doughnuts and people, Angela Kay suggested that they list all of the activities to be accomplished on the big Post-it paper she had purchased. She was willing to be the scribe. She was shocked when the principal said, "I'm a middle school person, and using big white paper is too elementary for me. Let's have Janie take notes." Janie did, and everyone left the meeting wondering what had happened. Maybe the principal was just having a bad day.

At the next meeting, Randy, one of the more senior teachers remarked, "Today, it would be great to focus on teamwork because teamwork has always been our Number One Priority." The principal responded, "For me, getting the job done is *first* priority, *teamwork is second.*" Now the teachers were really confused. It appeared that this principal did not respect the teachers or the process. She steamrolled ahead and lost the respect and trust of the group. She could have built relationships and strengthened trust even if she didn't like the individuals and their ideas.

Honesty—You Have My Word, You Can Trust Me

Honesty builds trust. Once a leader lies, people lose trust in him. He ends up having to tell more lies that corroborate his first lie, and often cannot remember the series of lies he has told to substantiate the first lie. More than likely he will get caught. The consequences for lying are grave ones. Everything he says or does becomes suspect. Suspicion abounds. Word spreads like wildfire that he can't be trusted.

When a leader is honest, trust and relationships flourish. Honesty breeds trust, whereas dishonesty breeds contempt and suspicion. When a leader is honest in a tactful and caring way, teachers feel safe; they know what is going on, and they feel protected and supported. We emphasize tactful and caring because there will be times when you have to tell individuals things they may not like to hear. These may be related to tardiness, discipline, bullying, incompetence, disrespect, etc. These areas can be hard to deal with, and as a leader, teachers expect you to resolve these situations in a manner that demonstrates support, tact, caring, honesty, and safety.

When a leader is honest about what she knows or doesn't know and goes about improving her weaknesses, teachers see an example they may wish to emulate. Honesty is a vital part of trust. Here is an example. Lindsay, a young and dynamic principal, was approached by the second grade teachers who wanted her opinion, knowledge, and guidance about writing a grant to increase computer hardware and software in the school. Lindsay did not know how to write a grant and had never done so. She explained this to the teachers. She told them that she would do some investigating and would get back to them in three days. She called her immediate supervisor and got the information and guidance needed. She pursued the notion of collaborating with the college of education at a nearby university. She reported what she knew to the teachers. While Lindsay gathered information, so did the teachers. They researched possibilities online and located a number of possible funding sources. They wrote the grant and were funded a year later. As a result of their collective effort, their school secured 60 additional computers and accompanying software. She practiced what we talked about in Chapter 4; she didn't have the knowledge she needed, told her teachers that she would get it, and she followed through.

Lindsay is also the principal who talked honestly to her faculty about personnel matters. At their first faculty meeting she said, "Throughout the year there may be some matters that arise directly related to personnel. This is normal in any school. I want you to know that out of respect for all of you, these matters will not be discussed openly. I don't want you to think I am being dishonest by not divulging information. Morally, ethically, and by law I am not able to disclose personnel information. Honesty is important to all of us, so rest assured that any and all personnel matters will be confidential."

Lindsay's honesty helped to strengthen and maintain trust. There will be times that you cannot and should not disclose information. Faculty and staff need to know this upfront. You will be respected and trusted for protecting the rights of everyone and for your honesty.

Do You Really Care About Me?

Teachers and staff want to trust you and be trusted themselves. They want you to care about them. It is a fortunate leader who assumes a position in which teachers, staff, and administration trust one another. This is a key facet in a healthy culture in which people care for people. Or, conversely, you might be submerged in a school devoid of trust. In a toxic culture, you will really have to utilize all of the Connectors to build trust. This kind of environment makes your job tougher. In order to be successful, you must remember how critically important trust is. You must strive to do everything you possibly can to build and sustain trust.

In a trusting environment, teachers and staff can be themselves; they can safely be who they have been conditioned to be. Harm will not come from the leader. Because they feel safe, they are more amenable to possibilities and change. They tend to become more fluid, unconstrained, and more willing to go the extra mile. They are more likely to move into the "zone" discussed in our chapter on safety. They are more inclined to examine what they believe, what they have been conditioned to believe, and whether they want to change what they believe. Transformation is possible in a safe and trusting environment.

Exemplary trusted leaders have a sincere desire to care for their teachers and staff. They honor and value people. They ensure safety. They are conscious of how people are treated and treat the individuals with whom they work as they would like to be treated. They look out for people. They care by providing a safe and clean school. They are attuned to individuals' needs and work with the budget to make sure needs are met. They are protective of the teachers and the students. They are aware that teachers expect some bureaucracy, but ensure that teachers aren't plagued with excessive paperwork and classroom interruptions. These effective leaders constantly demonstrate their benevolence.

We offer the following suggestions that will assist you in establishing an environment of caring.

- *Greet everyone you see each day.* Ask each individual how he or she is doing. Listen to what they say when they respond to your questions. Offer help if needed.
- *Use their names when you greet them.* Saying "Hi, Angela Kay" or "How are you today, Angela Kay?" is so much more powerful than a mere "Hi" or "How are you?" Names are extremely personal and important. Saying a person's name connotes caring and recognition of another individual's importance. Just be careful not to overdo it. People who overuse names tend to be annoying.
- *Refrain from complaining.* It causes anxiety for the leader and for those who are listening. Besides, no one likes to listen to a complainer. Complaining doesn't help a situation. Teachers and staff need to know that you care and will try to resolve the situation rather than complain about it.
- *Don't engage in gossip.* Ask yourself what useful purpose gossip serves. Gossip gets you in trouble and your trustworthiness will be questioned.
- *Treat people the way you want to be treated.* An excellent principal we know has a unique way of caring for teachers. She will tell them, "I am always striving to demonstrate my caring. If I'm not treating you the way you want to be treated, and if I am not showing that I care about you, please let me know." Teachers do tell her, and they also demonstrate their caring for her. The principal also says, "I want us to treat each child as if he or she is our own son or daughter." She asks the following questions at faculty meetings: "How do we demonstrate our benevolence toward all students? How do we demonstrate that each student is important even if he is incorrigible and doesn't do his homework? How do we demonstrate we care when some parents don't?" Trust and caring are underscored and highlighted at her school.

A Cautionary Note

Following are three examples in which the presence of caring is questionable. The first example is one in which a punishment, often practiced by teachers, demonstrates their lack of caring.

Sometimes teachers keep students from going to the cafeteria during lunch as punishment. This kind of behavior demonstrates that the teacher is frustrated, angry, and doesn't have a solution for that which the student is being punished. Students do not trust teachers when this happens, and they do not trust the principal when he condones this type of teacher behavior. Besides, keeping students in the classroom during lunch is dangerous and illegal in many states. All sorts of things can happen ranging from accusations, to health issues, to increasing the negative behaviors, to being sued, etc. Students lose trust in the teacher's ability to teach and provide a safe and productive environment.

The second example demonstrates a district's misguided attempt to change gang-related behavior. Recently a school district passed a policy that requires students to put on a black jumpsuit if they don't wear district-approved clothing. These black jumpsuits resemble prison garb. This policy is enforced in grades five through 12. This says volumes about caring, respect and trust to fifth graders, all students in the district, parents, and the community. It makes one wonder how many will graduate from this particular school district. It also makes one wonder if the adults in the district wear professional clothing, i.e., slacks instead of jeans, ties and jackets, blouses, skirts, and suits. What might their dress code be?

In the third example, drastic measures are under way to force students to come to school. A county court has made a decision for students who are habitually truant. Students are required to wear tracking Global Positioning System (GPS) bracelets. Money, time, and effort will be dedicated to tracking these students instead of working with them. This gives one cause to pause.

Valuing Strengths

A leader lays the foundation for trust when he consciously looks for and values others' strengths. In Chapter 5 on Continuous Renewal, we discussed the need for leaders to find the good in everyone. When we do this, teachers and staff are more likely to trust us. Everyone has talents and strengths that should be tapped, appreciated, and accentuated.

Neil, a middle school principal, was asked by the assistant superintendent to plan and implement a two-day in-service for 100 middle and high school science teachers. He immediately solicited the help of his fellow principals who cochaired the in-service. He knew that one principal was great at budgets, one was an A-type who was scrupulous with details, another was skilled at putting together a great program, yet another had a positive rapport with central facilities. He valued their strengths.

Neil asked each of these principals to find six to eight teachers per school to help with the event. These were volunteers with specific strengths who, like the principals, would be given a chance to shine. Together they planned and implemented an in-service that was relevant to what teachers did in the classroom, which would enhance teachers' knowledge, and offer tools to assist students in science.

On their evaluations teachers expressed a strong desire for similar in-services in the future. Teachers were eager to practice and sustain what they had learned. The district agreed to do so. The assistant superintendent sent each principal and teacher involved in the planning a letter of appreciation, which was copied to the superintendent and the board. She emailed all 100 science teachers who attended, thanked them for attending, provided a rough draft of the next in-service, and solicited their input. Neil also wrote letters of appreciation to his fellow principals, and they wrote letters to the teachers recognizing their strengths. Everyone felt valued. Strengths were identified, elucidated, and extolled. Principals and teachers were ready to roll up their sleeves and plan the next in-service. Having a caring "can do" attitude and "I'm with you" attitude serves leaders well.

Leaders who care are trusted. Consider this scenario about Rick, another high school principal. Rick hired a first-year algebra teacher. She did an outstanding job the first semester and got along well with everyone. Word spread throughout the school that she was a tough teacher, required students to be on time, gave credit for participation in class, which meant students had to attend, and gave meaningful assignments. When students were absent for serious reasons, illness, death in the family, etc., she certainly understood. Students would say, "Ms. Panna is really tough, but when you leave her class you know algebra inside out."

In December, the principal got a call from some parents who said they didn't want their children in Ms. Panna's class because she was too hard and required too much work. After all, they said that their children had basketball, cheerleading, and a number of other activities during the week; this left little time for homework. The principal told them he would do some investigating.

Rick spoke to the chair of the math department, who agreed with the parents, and thought that Rick should switch the students to another class.

According to the math chair, Ms. Panna was the most stringent in the department. Jokingly he said, "Hey, she makes the rest of us look bad. You better do something, Rick, she's new."

The principal then spoke to Ms. Panna. She showed him her course plan, her assignments, and her class requirements. It was clear that she knew what she was doing. Rick explained this to the department chair and did not take any students out of her classes. Rick informed the parents of his decision. Ms. Panna was relieved that students were not removed, and that the principal had confidence in her knowledge and skills. He discussed this situation with her and the department chair only. Rick kept this matter confidential and told her that he had spoken only to the department chair and to her.

You can imagine what would have happened (a) if the principal had emailed the entire department and asked for their help, (b) if he had talked to the entire department behind Ms. Panna's back, (c) if he had allowed the students to switch teachers, and (d) if he had declared this situation a crisis because Ms. Panna's classes were small. Rick communicated with Ms. Panna; he supported her, insured her mental and emotional health, and demonstrated his competence as a leader. As a result, Ms. Panna's trust in Rick will continue to grow.

Respecting Privacy

Sometimes people need to retreat quietly into their own worlds and relish the solitude they find there. Other individuals might sit attentively at faculty meetings and not answer questions. This happens for reasons, and leaders must respect their privacy. When a teacher is asked a question and his response is, "I'll have to pass on this one," that is perfectly okay. He may mentally be in another place or listening and processing what is being said. He may be anxious about speaking in front of other teachers. He may be formulating the answer, or may not know the answer. His privacy should be respected.

We talked earlier in another chapter about the principal who asked teachers to tell the group one good thing that happened to them. It's okay, and teachers should be respected if they do not respond. Leaders should not make any assumptions and should not press any teacher to speak. Some teachers and staff may not want to share anything about themselves, their families, hobbies, travel, health, etc., and this too is perfectly okay. They will let you into their lives when they want to. The leader's job is to be respectful of each individual's need to be private, and at the same time, be friendly, supportive, and open to all.

Some individuals are naturally quieter than others. Some may be shy, or dealing with personal or health issues. We just never know. Leaders need to build relationships, but they all don't have to be the same; they have to be meaningful, purposeful, and sustainable.

Betrayal

As mentioned earlier, it takes substantial time and energy to be trusted and to trust. A leader who truly cares, communicates effectively, supports, and provides a safe environment for teachers and staff, invests himself in these individuals, and they in him. If a relationship has been developed, a person is willing to be vulnerable to the leader. The person allows the leader to enter her world. When this happens, the seeds of trust are being planted, and they must be nurtured. The person puts faith in the leader and is certain that the leader will not harm her. She comes to school knowing that she can be the person she has been conditioned to be, can confide in the leader, and can go to the leader for help and refuge. Trust connotes protection. Trust makes everything happen. Trust makes everything work. Trust is safety from harm.

Betrayal of trust is devastating because the person who has been betrayed feels violated by the leader. The same holds true when teachers, staff, students, or parents betray the leader. A person is usually stunned when betrayed. She cannot readily figure out what has been done to her. She can't readily find answers. She searches for reasons why she feels the way she does. She looks at the leader in a different way. She no longer believes that he will protect her. She has been shattered. She goes about life differently knowing she has trusted the leader, and this was not the prudent thing to do. She will be on guard and will watch her back from then on. Everything the leader does will be suspect. Everything the leader says will be suspect. She may forgive, but will probably never forget that she has been betrayed because the hurt cuts to her very soul. If the betrayal is too egregious, a leader may never be forgiven and the betrayal may never be forgotten.

You might say that is too dramatic. It's not. People who trust you expect that you will never engage in behaviors that will betray that trust. The consequences of betrayal are serious and can rapidly destroy a relationship. When you betray trust, things are not the same because the relationship has changed.

Perceived Betrayal

Another startling and sad part about betrayal is that there is always the possibility of what we call "perceived betrayal." Like betrayal, the consequences of perceived betrayal are just as daunting and grave. A leader may have a positive relationship with a teacher, an administrative assistant, a student, a parent, etc. All expect their relationships to be nurtured and hope that they will last a lifetime. And then . . . something is said or done causing one to *perceive* that he or she has been betrayed. There may have been things that led up to the perceived betrayal, or it may be just one action, one word, one sentence. For this person, this perceived betrayal is reality. She asks the same soul-searching questions as someone who has been betrayed; suspicion overshadows the relationship. Subsequently, the relationship changes and the person who perceived the betrayal will be on guard from this point forward.

Leaders need to be aware of the possibility of perceived betrayal. As leaders we are often in a hurry to get things done and move to the next project. Our intentions are probably good; we don't want to hurt anyone. We don't purposely intend to leave someone out, or say or do anything that could be misunderstood. We, therefore, must constantly and consciously be aware of our actions and their impact on others. "I just wasn't thinking," and, "I was in a frenzy about getting the project done," are excuses that usually don't work. In perceived betrayal or betrayal the consequences are the same.

We offer the following suggestions to help you avoid betrayal and perceived betrayal.

- *Never talk negatively about anyone.* Try to remember the old adage, "If you have nothing nice to say, don't say anything at all."
- *Think before you open your mouth.* Think before you act. Reflection helps us avoid serious blunders with those we care about and those with whom we work. Remember that every action has a reaction. Make sure you reflect so that your words and actions cause wanted results
- *Listen more than you speak.* Sometimes it is better not to talk at all. Listen more than you speak so that you hear what is actually being said and then decide if your comments are necessary.
- *Be positive rather than negative.* You don't want people to wonder if they should or shouldn't trust you. Life is much more pleasant working in a positive rather than a toxic school culture. Trust is much more likely to spread in this environment.
- *Stay away from negative people, their problems, their messes, and ugliness.* There is another old adage, "Tell me who your friends are, and I'll tell you who you are." Whether consciously or subconsciously, people

tend to question the trustworthiness of negative people. They make assumptions about negative people.

- *Be above board.* People are weary of sneaky people who do things behind another's back. People simply don't trust sneaky people.
- *Value others and their contributions.* Remember everyone is different. Each person will behave differently, but they have hearts and souls that can be touched and can be broken.
- Be *careful of what you say and do.* Don't do or say anything that you would not want plastered all over the front page of your local newspaper, USA Today, the Nightly News, or YouTube.
- *Don't share your personal problems at work.* If you are fighting with your spouse, having trouble with your children, having money or credit card problems, weight problems, car problems, etc., etc., keep these to yourself. These are personal problems that you own, and they should not be shared with coworkers or associates at work. People have a tendency to judge others quickly, and sometimes they judge cruelly and brutally. They may even think, "Well, she has treated me the same way she treats her husband so I'm not surprised that she is fighting with him." Or, even worse, the person may tell you this face to face. So, don't even go there. Keep your personal problems to yourself. Trust is more likely to happen when people aren't engaged in judging you for what goes on at home. No need to provide any ammunition.
- *Be careful of the following statements.* "This is just between you and me." "I know you will keep this confidential." "Can you keep a secret?" When you begin a conversation with one of these statements, your trustworthiness is automatically questioned. Besides, a person sometimes forgets that what you're telling them is confidential. So, be careful; statements like these can get you in trouble.
- *Never lie.* Dynamic and trusted leaders aren't liars. They let people know when they are not at liberty to divulge information. When asked if you are aware of or know something you do not want to divulge you might consider saying, "Yes, but I really don't want to talk about it and get myself and my school involved. It would not be productive."
- *Apologize.* If you have betrayed another's trust or another perceives that you have betrayed him, apologize. Never repeat that action. Strive to never give the other person any reason to believe that it is possible to hurt him or her again.

Conversations with the Reader

A Walk on the Bright Side

Now it's your turn. Read the following story, and reflect on the ways **Leadership Connector, Trust** is demonstrated. See the questions at the end of this story to guide your reflection.

Mary

Do you remember Mary in Chapter 2, the new middle school principal who was supportive and successful at garnering the trust of teachers, staff, and students? Well, here is a story about her in her second year. She committed a major faux pas and could have lost everything she worked for in her first year. The following is what she did one Monday morning.

Mary returned from her morning walk-through. The substitute administrative assistant told her that someone called about an exciting dance and singing group that she was sure the middle school students would enjoy. Increasing assemblies for the students was one of Mary's goals this particular year. When she returned the call, she wasn't focused. She was concentrating on another project and should have paid much more attention to the woman on the other end of the phone. Mary heard, "We are members of a non-profit dancing and singing group named the Marching Turnaround Cadets, and we offer free assemblies to schools. We focus on ways in which students can get their lives on track, change their lives even if they had a challenging childhood, and grow to become productive students." Mary thought this would be an assembly that students would enjoy. Many came from home lives that were challenging. She scheduled the assembly for the following Thursday. She put flyers in the teachers' mailboxes and around the school and announced the upcoming assembly over the public address system for the next few days.

Thursday came, and so did the Marching Turnaround Cadets! Mary heard them in the halls and proceeded to the gym. All 1,359 students came and sat in their assigned bleachers with their homeroom teachers.

When the cadets marched in, they looked more like soldiers, even prisoners! Each was carrying a fake rifle, and they were marching and singing. When they finished their first number, the captain said, "Good afternoon, boys and girls and teachers. We would like to thank you and your principal, Mary Hampton, for inviting us to your school today. We have a great show for you but before we begin, I want to point out that each of the cadets you see in front of you is a reformed felon. They have all completed their prison sentences and are now out visiting schools to let kids know that you can change your life if you want to. Each cadet is in the process of changing. They do not want to return to prison. Please sit back and enjoy the show."

At this time Mary was gasping for air. Convicts in her school! What had she done? Her plan was to get them out of there as fast as she could. She looked around the gym and saw the teachers' eyes were all on her!

Then what she thought was the impossible happened! The captain said, "We would like all of you to come out of those bleachers, come to the floor, and dance with us." Before Mary knew what happened, all 1,359 students were stampeding out of the bleachers. They were screaming, jumping, pushing, shoving, punching, and everything else one might expect of middle school students in this situation.

Mary went immediately to the microphone and instructed the students to return to the bleachers. They didn't listen. She then let out loud pleas for the teachers' and staff's help. After five minutes, the teachers had them corralled and returned to their homerooms. The dismissal bell rang ten minutes later. Thank goodness! When the buses were gone, she asked all teachers and staff to come to the library for an emergency meeting. You should have seen their faces when they walked in. Some faces were full of anger, some bewildered, some shocked, and others were smiling.

When all were seated she began the meeting with, "I'm sorry. I'm very sorry for what happened in the gym today. You trusted me to pick an assembly by myself, I did so, and it turned out to be a complete disaster. *I was wrong*. Please let me try to explain where I messed up. When I returned the call to the captain of the Marching Turnaround Cadets, I wasn't listening to what she was saying. I heard what I wanted to hear. What I was saying in my mind and what I heard was, 'We don't have a lot of money budgeted for assemblies because we don't have a lot of money, this proposed assembly is free, and we'll all enjoy it.' How foolish of me. I am so sorry, I should have paid attention, I should have listened, and I broke the cardinal rule of not getting your input first. I'm sorry; I'll never do that again. Please find it in your hearts to forgive me."

When she was done, one of the angry teachers said, "That was really bad, Mary, don't pull that one ever again." Another said, "I was so worried that someone was going to get hurt." Another yelled, "Yeah, me!" And finally, the comments ended when another said, "Mary, you have taken good care of us, we still trust you. Thank you for saying you are sorry, let's just move on." She dismissed everyone ten minutes early that day and personally apologized to each as they left the room.

That afternoon she prepared a letter to the parents explaining what had happened, and she apologized. Parents called the superintendent the next day, outraged that their children wanted to be "just like the cadets!" They were furious that their children had to commit a crime in order to be part of the group. Superintendent Haisley got in his car and went to Mary's school. Mary explained the entire story and apologized profusely. Dr. Haisley understood and instructed her to never make such a foolish mistake again. He reminded her of systemic thinking and of what happens when you make a decision on your own that will impact everyone. She met with the entire school that day, talked about the group (she did so tactfully and respectfully), talked about appropriate behavior, and sent the letter home to parents.

It took Mary a few weeks to live this one down.

Reflective Questions

1. What happened?
2. What could have happened if Mary had engaged in reflection?
3. What is systemic thinking and why was it paramount in this story?
4. Why did Mary get the teachers and staff together right after the buses left?
5. Why did she have to apologize so many times? What if this had been her first year at the school?
6. Describe how she garnered trust by being honest and admitting she was wrong.
7. Why did things work out with the superintendent? Delineate and discuss each reason.

Our Analysis

Mary had good intentions. She knew that funds were lacking for assemblies. She listened to the substitute administrative assistant and returned the call to the Marching Turnaround Cadets. Then she made her mistake. She wasn't focused on what she was doing. She listened to what the captain of the Marching Turnaround Cadets was saying, but she really didn't hear her. She didn't ask enough questions, she didn't seek input from the leadership team; she made a snap decision and in came the cadets! She did not do her homework. She should have known everything about the cadets. She should have framed this assembly in a positive light. She should have emphasized and highlighted that it is possible to turn one's life around. It would have been wise of Mary to request that one of the cadets speak to the students about the consequences of gangs and crime. This cadet could have explained why students should not get involved in crime in the first place. Pandemonium erupted in the gym as one would expect because Mary was not reflective.

When the cadets were finished with the show, Mary should have gone to the microphone immediately. Instead, the captain proceeded to invite the students down on the gym floor to dance. She was lucky that the teachers helped and got the students back to their rooms.

Mary was wise to call a meeting as soon as all students were on the buses. This alleviated any time for teachers to congregate in a huddle to discuss the disaster. Mary did what a wise leader should do when something of this magnitude occurs; she apologized profusely, admitted she was wrong, and vowed that it would never happen again. She realized that she should not have made a decision that would impact everyone in the school without the leadership team. Systemic thinking, recognition that everything that occurs in the school impacts everything else in the school in some way, was reinforced in her discussion with the superintendent. She knew he was right.

Mary wrote a letter to the parents, answered calls from outraged parents, and met with students the following day. She knew that she needed to rebuild and fortify numerous other bridges.

Mary had focused on communication, safety, support, competence, respect, and trust the previous year. She knew that she would need to be much more focused and reflective. She would not jeopardize the relationships she had developed again. She learned her lesson! They forgave her. They appreciated Mary's willingness to say that she had made a mistake and she was wrong.

A Walk on the Dark Side

Now read the next story and reflect on what went awry. See the questions at the end of this story to guide your reflection.

Danny

Robert Walter High School has an enrollment of over 3,000 students. It is one of the largest high schools in the state. Because of its size, there are four assistant principals and one principal. The newest assistant principal, Danny Elias, was hired because of his success at a neighboring high school.

During the second year at Robert Walter, the principal made the decision to retire. The superintendent supported Danny's desire to apply for the principalship. Two of the other assistant principals, Greg and Marlene, had applied for jobs as principals in the district, but neither had been successful. They were bitter that they had been overlooked. Greg and Marlene were married to each other, and this was awkward at times in the work environment, but they had become friends with Danny.

During the previous two years, Danny developed a great rapport with Greg and Marlene. Their families would invite each other over for dinner, they went on weekend trips together, went to conferences together, and even exchanged gifts at Christmas time. They shared personal stories, confided in one another and had what Danny thought was a supportive and trusting relationship. Danny was pleased that he was part of Robert Walter High and part of a hardworking and dedicated group of colleagues. The work there was challenging as were the parents; however, Danny would go home and tell his wife how much he appreciated Greg and Marlene's friendship at school and in their personal lives. His wife remarked on numerous occasions that they were lucky to find people at the school who could be trusted.

At the end of that second year, Danny did apply for the principal's position. Danny sailed through the interviews. He had been at Robert Walter for two years and had served as an assistant principal for six additional years at another large high school. He had excellent evaluations; students and teachers liked him. He was described as a leader who could be trusted. The people at central office liked him; he was respected for his willingness to go above and beyond the call of duty. People in the school and in the district sought his input and help. He loved his job, and he did it well! On top of all of this, Greg and Marlene were his trusted friends; he knew he could count on them.

Marlene had told Danny numerous times over the past year to slow down. He was working harder than anyone else. Many times she would say, "Danny, you need to learn to say no. You are doing too much. You're in charge of graduation, and the district sponsored dinner to celebrate high school students. We have learned to say no, and we're kind of proud of that." Danny knew this, but he had a strong work ethic and loved every minute of what he did. He volunteered for many district committees, and his name was always suggested when the superintendent or associate superintendent needed something done or something spearheaded at the high school level. Greg and Marlene continued to remind Danny that he needed to learn how to say the word *no*. It crossed Danny's mind a couple of times that Greg and Marlene might be jealous of his success in the district, but he banished those thoughts because, after all, they were his good friends and colleagues.

After the interview process concluded in late June, Danny was at the high school working on the master schedule. Greg was working on book orders, and Marlene was working with Danny. He was wondering when he would hear the outcome of the process. That morning he received a call from the superintendent's office asking him to come by after lunch. The superintendent sounded enthusiastic.

When Danny told Marlene, he was surprised that she asked him if they could go for a walk. Danny obliged and was happy to get away from the master schedule for a while. As Marlene and Danny were walking, she said, "Danny, I have something to tell you, and I don't want you to be upset. Greg and I decided not to recommend you for the principal's job. We really had our hands tied. You know that Gabe was on the committee, and he wields a lot of power at Walter since he is the most veteran teacher. He insisted that since you had only been at Robert Walter for two years, you weren't ready to lead a large high school. We tried to convince him, but we knew we had no political choice but to go along with him. You are a great assistant principal Danny, and we understand how you feel. We have been passed over in the past, too. We just had no idea things would turn out this way."

Danny was more than shocked. He was overwhelmingly hurt. He was overwhelmingly angry. How could his friends and trusted colleagues not support him? How could they hurt him so badly? How could he ever go to their house again? How could he ever let them cross his threshold? How could they go along with Gabe who wasn't respected by anyone at the school? The emotional pain took over his entire body.

Danny got in his car and drove around for a while. He reflected on the past two years. He trusted Greg and Marlene. Why did Greg and Marlene volunteer to be on the committee? Did they volunteer to make sure that he didn't get it?

Danny went to the superintendent's office that afternoon. He was quite forlorn. When he walked in, Dr. O'Rourke said, "Congratulations, Mr. Elias, you are the new principal of Robert Walter."

"But . . ." said Danny. "Marlene told me that she, Greg, and Gabe did not recommend me." Dr. O'Rourke replied, "They don't know what they're doing. You're in; let me know what I can do to make your transition a smooth one."

Danny's relationship with Greg and Marlene was never the same. Danny was hurt, on guard, and always suspicious of their words and actions. They would not be given the opportunity to betray him again.

Reflective Questions

1. Describe Danny's relationships with Greg and Marlene.
2. Describe Danny's career path and his relationships with individuals in the school and district.

3. Describe the signals that were being sent.
4. What worked in this situation? How was trust developed?
5. What went wrong? What would you have done differently?
6. What surprised you in this story? What puzzled you? How would you handle being betrayed?
7. Describe the personal emotions that you experienced when you read this story?
8. If you had a chance to speak to Danny, what would you say?

Our Analysis

The analysis of this story is difficult and tricky. From a developmental perspective it was natural for Danny Elias to seek out friendships with fellow assistant principals. We all yearn for the safety and support that colleagues at work can provide. We all strive for the psychological success that we have discussed throughout the book. We all want to trust and be trusted.

In this particular story, Danny and his wife became too involved with Danny's co-workers, Greg and Marlene. The Elias family shared too much of their personal lives with them. Danny counted on Greg and Marlene's support. He did not pay attention to the signals his colleagues were sending. Greg and Marlene had not been able to get principal positions. They had been overlooked numerous times. Marlene frequently told Danny to slow down, not work so hard, and learn to say "No." Danny did not realize that they were in constant competition with him.

Greg and Marlene volunteered to be on the search committee. This gave Danny a false sense of hope. Danny was blind-sided. He never expected to be betrayed by Greg and Marlene. Marlene's explanation of having to politically support Gabe was very weak.

Danny was devastated. He mentally went through all of the questions that one would expect when betrayed. "Why? How did this happen?" His soul-searching was extraordinarily painful as was the betrayal.

Danny did get the job. His relationships with Greg and Marlene changed drastically. He was on guard and suspicious of their words and actions. These relationships were destroyed and would never be rescued.

It's Your Turn

Now, we invite you to think about a situation in your experience in which **Leadership Connector, Trust** seemed to be strong or weak. You may wish to record your thoughts in a journal. Writing can help you think in more detail and focus, revealing truths you have not seen before. Or you may wish to reflect on the situation with a trusted friend to ask you clarifying questions and to summarize what he or she hears you say. The following questions and statements may help you to focus your thinking.

1. Describe the situation you have selected in as much detail as you can.
2. Who was involved and what roles did they play? What role did you play?
3. Describe how you communicated with, supported, provided safety, demonstrated your competence and continuous renewal with the individuals involved.
4. Describe what you expected from them and what they expected from you.
5. What were the indicators that trust was being developed or thwarted?
6. What seemed to work well?
7. What could have been done differently to improve the outcome? In what ways were relationships built or destroyed?
8. Can broken relationships be rescued? If so, how? If not, why not?

Critical Points to Remember about *Leadership Connector, Trust*

- Trust is the most important part of any relationship; it is the most vulnerable and sensitive.
- Trust takes substantial time, energy, and commitment to the person or group whose trust a leader seeks.
- Trust is precious. It takes weeks, months, even years to develop and sustain.
- Trust can be destroyed in seconds, in just a word, in just a sentence, or in one action.
- We all come from unique backgrounds with unique ways of looking at people, of perceiving what is happening, and of evaluating how one fits into the overall scheme of things.
- We don't have to *like* everyone or *agree* with everyone; but as leaders, first and foremost we have to *respect* everyone.
- Exemplary trusted leaders have a sincere desire to care about their teachers and staff.
- A leader lays the foundation for trust when he looks for and values others' strengths.

- Betrayal of trust is devastating and has grave consequences.
- "Perceived Betrayal" is just as devastating as betrayal and has the same grave consequences.
- If you have betrayed another's trust or another perceives that you have betrayed him, apologize. *Never* repeat that action. Strive to *never* give the other person any reason to believe that it is possible to hurt him or her again.

Chapter 7

Putting It All Together

> May the road rise up to meet you, may the wind be always at your back,
> May the sun shine warm upon your face, and the rains fall soft upon your fields,
> And until we meet again, may God hold you in the palm of His hand.
> *Irish Prayer*

Throughout this book, we have examined the six **Leadership Connectors, Communication, Support, Safety, Competence, Continuous Renewal, and Trust.** Together we have explored how each connector relates to developing positive, meaningful, and lasting relationships for you and everyone at your school. We have also taken a deeper look into what happens when one of the connectors is missing or neglected in school relationships. When there is a disconnect, between or among the connectors, we as leaders become disconnected from teachers, staff, students, parents, and community. When a leader is disconnected, it is impossible to lead and to be followed. The journey is much more difficult.

What we wish for you is that you have been helped by reading this book, that you have had the chance to reflect on what you, as a leader, are doing, and, at the same time, you have been affirmed by all the good things you are doing. We celebrate you and your desire to continually renew yourself.

We end this book where we began in the introduction, with a story about Jeff, a remarkable first-year principal of a large, challenging high school. We ask you to fast forward to his retirement dinner 35 years later. This dinner celebrates his leadership journey.

Jeff's Retirement Dinner

Here it was Saturday, June 6th. Jeff could not believe that 35 years had passed so quickly. Where did the time go? When he accepted his first leadership position he was only 30. He couldn't fathom at that time that he would work in three different high schools over a 35-year period. Barker High was his first love. He learned so much there about teaching and learning. He learned even more about people and himself. He watched beginning teachers as they struggled to become their very best. He was truly blessed to see them develop into stellar teachers.

Initially he had not wanted to move on to Pfeiffer High, but could not pass up the chance to open a new high school. Things were easier it seemed because he didn't have to fight the resource battles he had fought at Barker. The budget was larger, it was a state-of-the-art new building, and he was able to become directly involved in selecting the faculty and staff. He made mistakes at Pfeiffer just as he had at Barker, but things always seemed to work out. He had great people to work with, and this made his job much easier.

His third position at Theresa Barry High School was his last. He was at Barker and Pfeiffer for 10 and 11 years, respectively, and his last 14 years at Barry were a great way to end his career. He had learned that the most powerful tool was reflection. He remembered very early on, the advice of his first superintendent who said, "Always remember to think before you speak and act. You don't have to always say or do something immediately. Give it a little thought, determine consequences and reactions, and then respond proactively." Jeff had always done that or at least tried to. When he didn't, it always got him in trouble. He also knew that in order for reflection to become intuitive, he had to work at the process. It wasn't easy; nevertheless, he had mastered the art after 35 years of focused practice.

At Pfeiffer and Theresa Barry, he consciously came to the realization that leadership was all about relationships. He worked hard at developing and sustaining relationships over the years. The people were the most important asset of any school, of any organization. He guided, facilitated, nurtured, and encouraged, but the students could have never excelled if it were not for the outstanding teachers and staff. Yes, it was all about relationships.

He had just finished adjusting the knot in his tie when he heard, "Honey, it's 5:30, are you ready?" Down the steps he went ready for his last hurrah.

He and his wife talked in the car, and Jeff noticed he was becoming more anxious. When he was at home just an hour ago, he was thinking about all the good things that had happened during his career. Then a dark cloud seemed to overshadow his thoughts. What if they thought about all the mistakes he made. He certainly had his share of gaffs and a series of unpleasant mistakes. Every time he had made an error he wasn't thinking clearly or wasn't thinking at all. Did those he hurt along the way forgive him? What could he have done differently? He felt nauseated; should he go home?

Before he knew it, they were in the parking lot at the restaurant. He tried to clear his thoughts. He walked into the restaurant and to his surprise, the room was packed. When the first person saw him, she started to clap and everyone else joined in. He made it through the crowd, shaking hands, hugging, and thanking each person for coming to his retirement party.

He saw teachers, staff, students, parents, fellow administrators, and friends that he was fortunate to know over the past 35 years. One student had traveled from Brazil to attend his dinner. Ari was now a CEO of a very successful electric company. Jeff remembered him being a handful when he was a student. Dianne, Katie, Ann, Patty, and Karen were there. He started his career with them and hadn't seen them for 17 years. Ginnie Sue, Kathy, and Tyler were there also, along with Russ, Julie, and Leroy. There was Nina, a former board member who supported his work at Pfeiffer. She was with Eva, another former board member.

After about 30 minutes everyone was seated, the superintendent welcomed everyone, and dinner was served. Jeff was happy that he was served a filet of beef. He had attended at least one retirement party per year for the last 35 years, and they always served chicken.

When everyone was almost finished with dessert, the superintendent got up and gave a heartwarming account of Jeff's career as an administrator in the district. A million thoughts were going through Jeff's mind. When the superintendent was finished, he asked if there was anyone in the audience who would like to say something. Jeff watched as people got up from different tables and approached the front of the room. The first to speak was Katie from Barker.

> Jeff, I don't know where to begin. We met 35 years ago when you first became a principal. How fortunate we were to have you as our leader! When we didn't know what we were doing, you did! When we said we couldn't do something, you assured us that we could and that we were capable of great things! When we said it wasn't worth it, you showed us the value in what we were doing! When we said we weren't smart enough, you reminded us of how much we really did know. Thanks, Jeff, for all you did for me and everyone at Barker.

Jeff's eyes welled up, and as he looked to his left, he saw Russ approach the microphone. Russ was one of the best counselors Jeff had ever worked with. He understood the kids at Barker and all the challenges that their home lives presented. Russ began,

> Wow, Katie that was really one of those "fuzzy" or whatever they are called, kind of stories. Jeff, do you remember the time that Tommy's dad tried to strangle you? Or the time Glenn's mother reached over your desk to choke you? I do! Everyone thought you were so brave, even the police did, but not everyone knew that you almost wet your pants that day, almost wet them twice! Sorry to tell everyone, Jeff. I didn't want everyone to think you were some kind of hero or saint or something. All kidding aside man, it was great working with you.

Next was Karen, from Pfeiffer High.

> Jeff, you always made me feel proud to be a teacher. You would tell the students in my classes and in the halls how lucky they were to have me as their history teacher. I'm not sure any of them believed you when you told them that I was your teacher, since I was only 28 at the time. And by the way, I don't think they believed you when you told them I knew so much about World War II because I was alive then! Thank you for making me feel good about being a teacher. You're the best!

Next was Patty, Jeff's first administrative assistant. When she got to the microphone, she paused and looked at Jeff for a full minute and then began:

> Jeff, my dear Jeff. How can I ever thank you? When my headaches started you were patient with me. I wondered then if you thought I was faking the pain. You had me lie down in Nurse Rita's office, you covered for me in the front office, you had Nurse Rita monitor me. Over the next two weeks you understood when I stayed home because the headaches became much worse. Then came that Wednesday morning when I passed out at my desk. You called the ambulance and knowing that my husband, Ken, was out of town, you followed the ambulance. When they decided to airlift me by helicopter to Cleveland Clinic, you were with me. That was 19 years ago. I made it through my brain surgery and I'm still cancer free. Thanks, Jeff, for being you.

When Patty left the microphone you could hear a pin drop. Jeff's impact on Patty and her family was felt by everyone.

Next to the microphone was George, one of the custodians from Barry High. His comments were very brief.

> Hey, Jeff, do they know that you like a bottle of beer now and then, that you eat three Snickers bars a day, and that you can't golf worth a damn? Well, anyhow, we still like you.

Four more people made similar comments about Jeff and then the big surprise came.

Ginnie Sue approached the microphone. She was one of the outstanding music teachers at Pfeiffer. She was a new teacher when the school opened and was there for the 11 years that Jeff was there. She then went on to become an assistant principal and principal of one of the district's high schools. Jeff remembered her fondly because when he left Pfeiffer, she organized an assembly for all of the students and teachers. At this farewell assembly students, faculty, and staff sang a song Ginnie Sue composed and wrote. Then a group comprised of 11 teachers, students, and staff went up to Jeff. Each gave him a red rose for each year he had been at Pfeiffer. Jeff never forgot this farewell and thought about it many times over the years.

Here was Ginnie Sue at the microphone once again. She spoke of the many relationships he had built over the last 35 years. And then, the most remarkable thing happened. Ginnie Sue asked 35 people to come to the front of the room. She sat at the piano and started to play the song "All Along the Way" that she had written for him years before. The words were as follows:

All along the way
You gave us more than just a moment
Now I want to say
You gave it all without a warning
Now I think I see
What could really be
And you gave us the strength
To turn dreams into reality

All along the way
You've been a friend
Through joy and sorrow
Now I want to say
You gave us hope to face tomorrow
Now I think I see
What could really be

And you gave us the strength
To turn dreams into reality

All along the way
You gave it all without a warning
You gave us more than just a moment

When they finished the first song, Ginnie Sue began the music for the song, "The Wind Beneath My Wings." When the group sang the last three lines:

Thank you, thank you,
Thank God for you,
The wind beneath my wings,

the entire room full of people gave Jeff a standing ovation. When everyone sat down, each of the 35 people took a red rose from the box on the table next to them and handed each rose to Jeff. These 35 roses represented his 35-year career.

Jeff got another standing ovation. It was his turn to speak. He approached the microphone wiping tears from his eyes. He carried all 35 roses with him. He spoke for a few moments and told them that over the past 35 years, he had learned that leadership was all about relationships. He thanked them for giving him the chance to be part of their lives and he a part of theirs. He closed by asking them to remember what Christopher Robin said to Pooh, in *Pooh's Great Adventure.* Jeff quoted Christopher.

If ever there's a tomorrow when we're not together
There's something you must remember...
You're braver than you believe and stronger than you seem,
And smarter than you think, but the most important thing
Is even if we're apart, I'll always be with you.

Recommended Reading

The Sources of Our Inspiration

The inspiration in this book came from our collective 74 years in education, our conversations with hundreds of leaders, some outstanding leaders that have led us, and many great teachers and staff members with whom we have been fortunate to work.

Over the years, we have read many books and articles that have impacted our thinking and how we developed relationships. The following list is by no means an exhaustive one. There is a plethora of outstanding books out there about leadership. We have cited the authors in the text; they are listed below along with other books and articles we recommend to you. These have inspired us and guided our thinking.

Axelrod, A. (2000). *Elizabeth I CEO: Strategic Lessons from the Leader Who Built an Empire*. Paramus, NJ: Prentice Hall.

Bennis, W., & Goldsmith, J. (1997). *Learning to Lead: A Workbook on Becoming a Leader*. Reading MA: Addison Wesley.

Bercholz, S., & Kohn, S. C. (1993). *An Introduction to the Buddha and His Teachings*. New York: Barnes & Noble.

Bridges, E. M. (1998). *The Incompetent Teacher: Managerial Responses*. Philadelphia: Falmer.

Burmeister, L., & Hensley, P. A. (2004). It's All about Leadership. *Leadership*, 30–31.

Collins, J. (2001). *Good to Great*. New York: Harper Business.

Covey, S. R. (1990). *The 7 Habits of Highly Effective People: Powerful Lessons in Personal Change*. New York: Simon and Schuster.

Covey, S. R., Merrill, A. R., & Merrill, R. R. (1994). *First Things First: To Live, to Love, to Learn, to Leave a Legacy*. New York: Simon & Schuster.

Covey, S. R. (2004). *The 8th Habit: From Effectiveness to Greatness*. New York: Free Press.

Csikszentmihalyi, M. (2004). *Good Business: Leadership, Flow, and the Making of Meaning*. New York: Harper & Row.

Davis, S. H., & Hensley, P. A. (1999). The Politics of Principal Evaluation. *Journal of Personnel Evaluation in Education*, 13(4), 383–402.

Dingfelder, S.F. (2006). Banishing Bullying. Monitor on Psychology, 37 (7). Retrieved January 26, 2007, from http://www.bullyinginstitute.org/apamonitorA0706.html.

Ferrucci, P. (2006). *The Power of Kindness: The Unexpected Benefits of Leading a Compassionate Life.* New York: Penguin.

Frase, L., & Hetzel, R. (1990). *School Management by Wandering Around.* Lancaster: Technomic.

Fullan, M. (2008). *The Six Secrets of Change: What the Best Leaders Do to Help Their Organizations Survive and Thrive.* San Francisco: Jossey-Bass.

Fulton, R. (1995). *Common Sense Leadership: A Handbook for Success as a Leader.* Berkeley: Ten Speed Press.

Glickman, C. D., Gordon, S. P., and Ross-Gordon, J. M. (2005). *The Basic Guide to SuperVision and Instructional Leadership.* Boston: Pearson, Allyn and Bacon.

Goleman, D., Boyatzis, R. & McKee, A. (2002). *Primal Leadership: Realizing the Power of Emotional Intelligence.* Boston: Harvard Business School.

Goleman, D. (2006). *Social Intelligence: The New Science of Human Relationships.* New York: Random House.

Hensley, P. A. (1996). *The Recognition and Legitimization of Female Superintendents as a Diverse Group Whose Husbands Have a Direct Impact on Job Performance, Acceptance, and Retention.* Unpublished Doctoral Dissertation, State University of New York, Buffalo, New York.

Hensley, P. A. (2006). Chapter 10: Organizational Culture, Relationships, Induction and Reflection. In D. Erickson & L. Wildman (Eds.), *Quality School Leadership Begins with Quality Preparation Programs: Professors of Educational Administration and Their Students' Professional Administrative Practice*: Association of California School Administrators.

Hensley, P. A., & Burmeister, L. (2004). The Artistry of Communication. *Leadership*, 30–33.

Hensley, P. A., & Burmeister, L. (2006). Effective Discipline: Finding the Place in the Middle. *Leadership*, 26–29.

Hensley, P. A., & Burmeister, L. (2008). School Improvement and Trusting Relationships: Connecting Theory to Practice. *School Leadership Review.*

Hoy, W. & Miskel, C. (2007) *Educational Administration: Theory, Research, and Practice.* New York: McGraw Hill.

Hoy, W.K. & Tarter, C.J. (2004). *Administrators Solving the Problems of Practice: Decision-Making Concepts, Cases, and Consequences.* Boston: Pearson.

Johnson, S. (1984). *The Precious Present.* New York: Doubleday.

Kidd, S. M. (1995). *The Dance of the Dissident Daughter: A Woman's Journey from Christian Tradition to the Sacred Feminine.* San Francisco: Harper San Francisco.

Kidd, S. M. (2006). *When the Heart Waits: Spiritual Directions for Life's Sacred Questions.* New York: Harper Collins.

Lord, R. G., Klimoski, R. J., & Kanfer, R. (Ed.). (2002). *Emotions in the Workplace: Understanding the Structure and Role of Emotions in Organizational Behavior.* San Francisco: Jossey-Bass.

Loughran, J. (1996). *Developing Reflective Practice: Learning About Teaching and Learning Through Modeling.* Washington, D. C.: Falmer Press.

Maxwell, J. C. (1993). *Developing the Leader Within You.* Nashville: Thomas Nelson Publishers.

Meyers, L. (2006). Still Wearing the Kick Me Sign. *Monitor on Psychology,* 37(7). Retrieved January 26, 2007, from http://www.bullyinginstitute.org/apamonitor B0706.html

Meyers, L. (2006). Worrying for a Living. *Monitor on Psychology,* 37(7). Retrieved January 26, 2007, from http://www.bullyinginstitute.org/apamonitorA0706.html

Milne, A. A. (1997). *Pooh's Great Adventure, the Search for Christopher Robin.* New York: E. P. Dutton.

Morgan, A., & Lynch, C. (2006). *Leading from the Front: No Excuse Leadership Tactics for Women.* New York: McGraw Hill.

Nouwen, H. J. M. (2005). *With Open Hands.* Notre Dame, IN: Ave Maria Press.

Pajares, F. (2002). Overview of Social Cognitive Theory and of Self-Efficacy. Retrieved August, 19, 2008 from http://www.emory.edu/EDUCATION/mfp/eff.html.

Pausch, R. (2008). *The Last Lecture.* New York: Hyperion.

Piper, W. (1930). *The Little Engine That Could.* New York: Platt and Munk.

Schmieder, J. H., & Cairns, D. (1996). *Ten Skills of Highly Effective Principals.* Lancaster: Technomic.

Senge, P., Scharmer, C. O., Jaworski, J., and Flowers, B. S. (2005). *Presence: An Exploration of Profound Change in People, Organizations, and Society.* New York: Currency.

Senge, P. M. (2006). *The Fifth Discipline: The Art & Practice of the Learning Organization.* New York: Currency.

Seyfarth, J. T. (2001). *Personnel Management for Effective Schools.* Boston: Allyn and Bacon.

Shaw, R. B. (1997). *Trust in the Balance: Building Successful Organizations on Results, Integrity, and Concern.* San Francisco: Jossey-Bass.

Smith, G. P. (1997). *The New Leader: Bringing Creativity and Innovation to the Workplace.* Delray Beach FL: St. Lucie Press.

Solomon, M. (1990). *Working with Difficult People.* Paramus, NJ: Prentice Hall.

Stambor, Z. (2006). Bullying Stems from Fear, Apathy. *Monitor on Psychology,* 37(7). Retrieved January 26, 2007, from http://www.bullyinginstitute.org/apamonitor A0706.html

Sutton, R.I. (2007). *The No Asshole Rule: Building a Civilized Workplace and Surviving One That Isn't.* New York: Warner.

Tschannen-Moran. (2004). *Trust Matters: Leadership for Successful Schools.* San Francisco: Jossey-Bass.

Those Who Can, Do. Those Who Can't, Bully. Retrieved January, 23, 2007 from http://www.bullyonline.org/workbully

Wheatley, M. (2004). Making Time to Think and Reconnect. *ASCD Education Update*, 46(4), 8.

9781596671065